Galloway of Buraan

GALLOWAY *of* BURAAN

E. M. CLIFFORD

RESOURCE *Publications* · Eugene, Oregon

GALLOWAY OF BURAAN

Copyright © 2022 E. M. Clifford. All rights reserved. Except for brief quotations in critical publications or reviews, no part of this book may be reproduced in any manner without prior written permission from the publisher. Write: Permissions, Wipf and Stock Publishers, 199 W. 8th Ave., Suite 3, Eugene, OR 97401.

Resource Publications
An Imprint of Wipf and Stock Publishers
199 W. 8th Ave., Suite 3
Eugene, OR 97401

www.wipfandstock.com

PAPERBACK ISBN: 978–1–6667–3617–5
HARDCOVER ISBN: 978–1–6667–9416–8
EBOOK ISBN: 978–1–6667–9417–5

FEBRUARY 28, 2022 1:16 PM

In memory of my father

He that soweth to the Spirit shall of the Spirit
reap life everlasting
Let us not be weary in well doing
for in due season we shall reap, if we faint not
As we have therefore opportunity, let us do good unto all
especially unto them who are of the household of faith
—GALATIANS 6:8-10

Preface

The first question in your mind probably should be, "Buraan? Where is that?" The ancient Sumerians knew the river Euphrates by its prehistoric Ubaid name: *Buranun*. From its origin in the mountains of what is now eastern Turkey near Erzurum, the Euphrates courses more than 1700 miles all the way across Mesopotamia to the Persian Gulf.

The civilizations and language groups that occupied this region since 7000 BCE were many and varied, changing radically over time. The land area that forms the fictional nation of Buraan includes the Roman province of Cilicia, the medieval Crusader state of Edessa, and just a bit more and less. Recall that the modern borders of nations and states in the Middle East were created by a chaotic political and military process that one may observe is still going on.

The action of this novel takes place during two eventful weeks, one in March 1910 and the other in September 1925. During this historical period, the area described was simultaneously Armenia, Kurdistan and Turkey, depending on whom you asked. At least eight languages were in daily use there. It was Christian, Muslim, Jewish, Yezidi, Druze. It was Sunni, Shi'ite and Sufi. It was Roman Catholic, Protestant, Greek Orthodox, Assyrian Orthodox, Armenian Orthodox. Generally there was a productive coexistence, albeit with friction, among all of these identity groups. At times, there was not.

This novel centers upon the Rev. David Simcox Galloway, an American Presbyterian educator and clergyman, missionary to Buraan. He and his colleagues, both foreign and indigenous, experience many of the pressures characteristic of the times, and certain exceptional ones as well.

Preface

Much of the literature portraying missionary life and work in the nineteenth and early twentieth centuries tends to deal in simplistic categories and stereotypes that fail to do justice to the historical record. I intend to represent post-colonial critiques of mission while also embodying the way Christians of the time lived their faith, expressed themselves, and observed the norms of their social context. The novel tells an engaging personal story while digging into issues of intercultural encounter, indigenous agency, vernacularization, interfaith relations, gender roles in mission, the advent of modernity, mission philanthropy in that era, and the effects of imperialism in the Middle East. David Galloway reconsiders many of his assumptions over the time span of this story.

The accuracy of the period detail involved is important to me. I have always admired the Aubrey and Maturin series by Patrick O'Brian, beginning with *Master and Commander*. His ability to weave massive amounts of scrupulously researched information about the Royal Navy of 1790–1820 into dramatic and richly populated narratives serves as a model.

Primary source materials are the bedrock for this work. For example, information about the method of copying handwritten texts comes from a technical manual for library practices published in 1903. The proposal for establishing an American Mission college is based upon a prospectus for the Central Turkey College in Aintab; other important information about mission schools of that era comes from contemporary documents of the Syrian Protestant College in Beirut, Robert College in Constantinople, Assiut College in Egypt, the Tripoli Boys' School in what is now Lebanon, and several sources detailing the work of Calvin Mateer and Timothy Richard in China. Medical procedures were derived from dated information available at the time, such as a medical manual widely used in 1910, and a newsletter for retail pharmacists published in 1909. The racist attitudes of J. Gresham Machen are documented by his own words, from letters written to his mother in 1913. Rites and public prayer in the mission churches are taken nearly verbatim from *The Book of Common Worship* of the Presbyterian Church in the United States of America published in 1906; information about the history of sacred music and hymnody is accurate as well.

Other information has been adapted with greater liberty. The Hanamid faith and its practices are based upon the Yezidi tradition of Syria and

Preface

Iraq, as well as Zoroastrian customs in Persia. They are viewed primarily as Protestant Christian missionaries might have understood them in the early 1900s. The catastrophic persecution of Armenians in the Ottoman era is drawn from first-person accounts, news and media articles, diplomatic reports, professional memoirs and academic publishing, but fictitious individuals have been added to known scenarios. The stories of Shueyda Momonen and his collaboration with David Galloway are based loosely upon the life and ministry of Vedanayagam Samuel Azariah of Dornakal and his association with Henry Whitehead and Sherwood Eddy. The eclectic and powerful musical tradition of the church in Buraan is derived from the mission legacy and the rich creativity of the Telugu Christians of South India, as well as the Evangelical churches of Egypt.

Most significantly, I have established a mission association that did not, in fact, exist: the American Mission in Buraan. The organization, staffing, funding and policy-making of the AMB are based upon the American Mission in Egypt, a unique and constructive undertaking of the United Presbyterian Church of North America (UPNA). Most of the Protestant missionaries in Syria and Turkey were actually attached to the American Board of Commissioners for Foreign Missions and their worldwide outreach.

My thinking has also been immeasurably enriched by the academic analysis of very high quality that is now current in the field of missiology. I became acquainted with many of the leading scholars in this field through the American Society of Missiology and the Association of Professors of Mission, attending their annual meetings, listening to their papers, reading their books, and absorbing their meticulously documented and nuanced understandings of the vivid and controversial history of all of the actors in this field. Several of their books and articles are listed among the "Selected Sources."

13–19 March 1910

Chapter 1

Sunday morning, deep in snow. Almost everyone in the village had been there for hours already, staying warm and being together, filling the small church. The sound of singing surrounded it like a cloud.

The building and compound were alive with children running about. Older people were sitting comfortably and chatting, men and women on opposite sides of the center aisle. The Lord's Day was the glowing heart of their week, a welcome respite from daily worry and toil.

The mission compound was established at the edge of the village, nearly surrounded by pine forest. In accordance with property transfer requirements in Buraan, the first structure built was a low stone wall delineating the edges of the parcel. There was a great deal of open space within the wall to allow for future expansion: perhaps a school, clinic or orphanage. But for now, there was only the handsome wooden church with its steeply-pitched shingled roof, and a parsonage or manse for the Reverend Asa McKinley, his wife Catherine, and their three young children, including a newborn baby. These sturdy buildings were the only ones with glass in the windows in the whole village of Kaskut.

That Sunday morning, Mrs. McKinley and the baby were quietly enjoying their postpartum solitude in the manse, while the church was thronged with people. The McKinleys were the key staff members of the American Mission in Buraan serving the Armenian-speaking villages of the Kaskut area. Subdued and sincere, the family blended smoothly into the Christian community, and their presence was much appreciated.

At half-past ten, Asa McKinley and the choir began the service of worship, which failed to quell the general disorder of the congregation but did begin to channel it in the right direction. The portable pump-organ was crude but loud, and all of the people loved singing. Catherine could hear the sound of it inside the manse even with the windows closed.

Kaskut was located well up in the Taurus Mountains in the Maziret district, near the border with Turkey, and in March it was still in the grip of winter. The snow was fresh.

A rustle among the long-needled pines resolved into many dark figures, all on horseback. Warmly dressed, heavily armed, with supplies following on pack animals. They moved with a minimum of disturbance into position, ringing the compound wall. Some appeared to be uniformed Ottoman military, but the majority wore ordinary garments—Turkish or Kurdish irregulars or collaborators from other towns, probably beyond the border. All of them evidently believed they had some justifiable grievance against the Armenian population.

"Oh come, let us worship and bow down; let us kneel before the Lord our Maker," Asa called out, opening the liturgy, translated into the language of the people. "Know ye that the Lord he is God. It is he that hath made us, and not we ourselves. We are his people, and the sheep of his pasture."

The standing people bowed their heads, most of them reverently, most of them silently. "Almighty God, who of thy great mercy hast gathered us into thy visible church, grant that we may not swerve from the purity of thy worship, but so honor thee, both in spirit and in outward form, that thy Name may be glorified in us, and we may be true members of thine only-begotten Son, Jesus Christ our Lord."

"Amen," responded the people, firmly.

An officer in the patrol nodded to a few of the irregulars, who urged their animals over the wall and close to the church. They packed rags of sackcloth along the sides of the church, brought out metal canisters full of liquid and began to pour it around the outside of the building, the doors and the steps. The smell of kerosene was pungent in the cold air.

Drawing back from the building, they looked to the officer again for a command. He made a sharp gesture, and they deployed themselves around the building, producing wooden friction matches in a coordinated manner. Matches lighted, they dropped them upon the heaps of sackcloth against the walls, and moved away.

Chapter 1

The wooden church took flame in seconds, and at that moment those inside realized that something was wrong. There was a commotion of people and furniture, voices rising, cries of panic, and the doors flew open to a wall of flame.

The officer gave another order, loudly this time, and the patrol leveled their weapons at anyone who was bold or frantic enough to escape. The crack of rifle shots. The marksmen picked off the able-bodied men first, but any others were fair game if they seemed able to get away. Dead and wounded littered the compound. The shrieks and cries from within the church rose into a single chorus of mortal terror.

Within the parsonage a little ways off, Catherine McKinley heard what sounded like gunfire, but to her the noises made no sense. Scrambling out of bed in her flannel nightgown, she rushed to a window, and clearly saw the church engulfed in flame.

Concentrating her mind with an effort, she scooped up the baby in her arms and tried to think of a place to hide, settling on the pantry. Reconsidering, she found her heavy overcoat, shoes and a blanket, then retreated to the pantry and closed them in.

Terrible sounds reached her even there. With despairing tears she prayed for her beloved Asa and their two older children—Anne, age seven, and Matthew, age five, who were certainly at the church that morning.

The operation was a very simple one for the soldiers, and did not take long. When it seemed clear that no one else would emerge from the church, they came over the wall on their horses and began to hunt down survivors.

Adults were finished off with a bullet. But the children required greater deliberation. They were one of the chief objectives of this raid. Children between the ages of four and ten—that is, old enough to travel without a lot of tedious attention, but young enough to be in demand from buyers. There were numerous children left, so they took the time to select the most desirable ones: healthy, good-looking, well-dressed in warm clothing. These they herded together into a terrified cluster and posted guard. Among them were Anne and Matthew.

In the pantry, Catherine began to feel trapped, just waiting for the killers to arrive. Perhaps she could bolt from the pantry and out through the kitchen door, run across the compound, climb over the wall, and escape into the pine forest. Collecting herself, she decided it was the only way.

She stumbled out the door and down the back steps just as some of the soldiers reached the parsonage. They had learned, from a lucrative career destroying Armenian villages, that the leader of the community almost always lived near the church and probably had some items of value in his home. So they took care not to burn the pastor's house but to search and pillage it instead.

Catherine plowed through the nearly knee-deep drifting snow in her long flannel nightgown, the baby pressed to her body. She gasped with terror and exertion. Before long, one of the soldiers spotted her and felled her with a single shot to the back.

As she fell headlong to the ground, the baby was flung from her arms. He landed some distance away from her, plunging into the snow. The soldiers ignored them both as they ransacked the house.

Having satisfied themselves that they had harvested everything of value from the manse, the unit prepared to leave. They took twenty-one children as contraband, distributing them upon their horses, with strict orders to them to hold on behind the rider if they wanted to survive.

They would need to carry the children across the Anatolian landmass to a variety of locations—far from Kaskut and the Maziret district, to places where they were very unlikely to be recognized—and find buyers for them who had every reason to keep silent about their origin. The children would be in demand as house servants, laborers, weavers, animal tenders, and for other purposes. The proceeds of their sale would compensate these collaborators, and the Turkish government could claim that their own soldiers were not guilty of such crimes against civilians. They had an important job to do, suppressing insurrection among the disloyal Armenian population.

For a few hours after they left, some tiny shuddering sounds could be heard from the bundle in the snow. The cry of an infant in the bitter cold. By the time the early dusk of March enveloped the mountains, it was quiet and motionless. Only a few were left to report the extinction of Kaskut.

Chapter 2

That same Sunday evening, the Reverend David Simcox Galloway was working late in his office, even though he was already tired after all of the services required for the Lord's Day. He would have liked nothing better than to sit beside his fire and relax for a bit.

There was a knock at the door: one-two, one-two. That would be Julius, using his distinctive knock.

"Come in, Julius, it's unlocked."

The Buraani porter and general maintenance overseer of the American Mission building stepped into Galloway's office. This dignified gentleman—well on in years, now—had received his nickname from a former AMB director. Julius, as in Julius Caesar, so called because of his imperious demeanor. Julius himself seemed to take great satisfaction in it.

"Beg your pardon, *ya mudeer*," said Julius, using an honorific, meaning *Director*. "I'll just be going off duty now. That young fellow Bocksi is on watch tonight. He'll also open in the morning, since I'm heading out early to my sister's in Ypli Dag for my holiday, if you recall."

"Oh yes, that should be fine. Thank you."

"Just between us, that Bocksi isn't the sharpest knife in the kitchen, if you follow me. But he ought to be able to bring you a glass of tea if you need it."

"I think I'll be fine here, Julius. Just need to get this work done before tomorrow."

"Very good then, *mudeer*. A blessed night to you."

"And to you. Also, have a pleasant holiday." Julius nodded gravely and departed.

Galloway was working on a deadline, as so often seemed to happen; as the head of the American Mission in Buraan, he inherited every problem that the other staffers found to be intractable, and all of the bureaucratic correspondence between Buraan and the church leadership in Pittsburgh depended upon him.

He also pastored the primary Presbyterian congregation in Adamu, the district capital, and held oversight responsibility for every other congregation belonging to the Mission, numbering some twenty-six properly established small churches so far. Almost all of these operated under lay leadership, as they had nowhere near enough missionary clergy to supply them all, and the formation and training of an indigenous Buraani pastorate was still in its early stages.

The Presbyterian church in Buraan was a relative latecomer to the Syrian and Turkish mission fields. Buraan was a neglected corner of the Ottoman Empire, used its own language that was little-known beyond its borders, and followed the obscure Hanamid faith for the most part. There were villages of Orthodox Christians, mainly Armenian. But Hanamids predominated, and responded with indifference to most attempts to introduce them to Christianity.

However, the founding of schools for young Buraani children was proceeding with much success. Parents were enthusiastic about the social advantages they expected a Western education to provide for their children. The Mission was teaching nearly two thousand children in towns and villages all over the country, mainly with willing but scarcely-trained indigenous teachers, under the direction of missionary ladies from Pennsylvania, Ohio, and Virginia, who had found their vocation in civilizing these young creatures, as they understood the task.

Galloway believed that the only way ahead for the Mission was to create a credible preparatory and secondary school, a "college" in normal parlance, capable of producing the pastors, teachers, doctors, and other professionals qualified to lead the formative Buraani church. The germ of this college now met under his own tutelage in a single room in the bottom of the Mission building. Other Mission staff helped to teach as they were able. But they needed a proper faculty, equipment, buildings, books. They

Chapter 2

needed a major capital investment. And it was Galloway's job somehow to make this happen.

Darkness had fallen long ago, and Galloway sat working in the single pool of light created by the heavy old oil lamp suspended over his desk. He could see just well enough to write. A prospectus for the founding of a new College for central Buraan was taking shape from a mass of drafts and data scattered across his desk.

Before he could embark upon a fair and final version of the document, he had to prepare a fresh batch of copying ink. This ink would dry slowly on the paper, allowing him to create an exact copy on his letter-press, so that he could send the original to Pittsburgh by personal courier and keep a copy at the Mission offices.

With great care, he measured eight ounces of hematine dye—an imported substance, very costly. To this he added a spoonful of ordinary alum, such as is used for pickling cucumbers, and a spoonful of table sugar. Then, he mixed in six ounces of glycerine, the key to making the ink the right consistency for copying. This ink needed to be used at once, as the glycerine would soon congeal into an unusable glue. He now had enough of this mixture for a multi-page document.

He had several newly-sharpened pens ready to use; choosing his favorite one, he began to write. *A Proposal for Establishing a Christian College and Medical School in Central Buraan*, he inscribed carefully. He was so conscious of writing legibly and confidently that in fact he caused his own hand to tremble.

The Local Board of Management and Trustees. Rev. David S. Galloway, Adamu. Rev. Asa McKinley, Kaskut. Felix Marshall, M.D., Adamu. Miss Louisa Booth, Osmaneyya. Mr. Manro Olorzey, Adamu. Board of Oversight in the United States. Rev. Samuel Casters, Pittsburgh. Mr. John Campbell Hardy, Pittsburgh.

David recognized that the support upon which he was relying was, so far, rather thin. He was hopeful that Reverend Casters at the headquarters of the United Presbyterian Church of North America, and the Presbyterian industrialist and benefactor J.C. Hardy, would soon be able to enlist further help, manpower, and funding.

It is proposed by the Presbyterian Church of Central Buraan, in connexion with the American Missionaries, to establish a Christian College in the district capital of Adamu. The primary object of this College will be the thorough education of young men for the Christian Ministry. In addition, it will furnish, at reasonable expense, the means for a good education to young men of all classes of Society, whose mother tongue is the Buraani language. It is designed as well to provide practical training in a Medical Department to prepare young physicians for practice within Buraan.

Manro Olorzey, a relatively wealthy landowner and the most prominent layman in the local Presbyterian community, was emphatic that medical training should be offered, although Galloway doubted that they would have the means of launching anything like an actual medical school in the foreseeable future. They had one missionary physician, Dr. Marshall, and he was not particularly interested in taking on such a responsibility at his age. Nevertheless.

The Syrian Protestant College in Beirut, the Central Turkey College in Aintab, Robert College in Constantinople, Anatolia College in Marsovan, and Assiut College in Egypt, all provide examples of what can be accomplished in this regard. As far as human instrumentality is concerned, they serve the need of each Country for a class of virtuous and well-educated Christian leaders. But they are far removed from Buraan both in physical distance and cultural knowledge, using Armenian, Turkish, Arabic or English as their medium of instruction. There is no comparable institution in existence to offer a proper education to upper-level students through the Buraani language.

David's reasoning seemed compelling to himself, but he was not sure that from Pittsburgh's vantage point the distinction would be so meaningful.

The course of study envisioned would cover four Collegiate and two Preparatory years, beginning at age twelve or thirteen. Students would receive a creditable education in the Sciences, Mathematics, History, Philosophy, Economics, Geography, Rhetoric, and of course the Christian Scriptures. Future departments of study might include Agriculture, Engineering and Law. Graduates would be prepared to move from the secondary level into Universities abroad, or directly into the professions for which they have received practical preparation.

Chapter 2

Galloway felt himself to be deficient in comparison to the leaders of peer institutions to the one he longed to establish, such as Charles Chapin Tracy of Marsovan, and John Hogg of Assiut. They had decades of progress to show for their efforts, while he was still at the starting point. He never thought to compare himself to the most eminent of international educators, such as Daniel Bliss of Beirut, or Timothy Richard of China.

But he recalled that Richard and his compatriot in China, Calvin Mateer, founder of Shantung College, had stressed the practical value of learning and ethical training for the youth of a nation as the engine of society's growth and the most efficacious means of bringing credit to the Gospel among unbelievers. Surely, they thought, ignorance and superstition lay at the basis of much of the chauvinism of the Chinese toward the West. Likewise, enlightened learning in Buraan would go far to moderate the resistance of the population to the influences now coming upon them, and since sound knowledge is the handmaid of true religion, it would ultimately draw them toward the Christian faith. "I am after the leaders," Richard once said. "If you get the leaders, you get all the rest."

As Dr. Tracy of Marsovan has so aptly observed, "Intelligent faith and efficient leadership are in perfect harmony with the New Testament idea of the evangelization of the world and the establishment of Christian society." Uplifting the minds of the Buraani people will ultimately cleanse them of the pollution of polytheism and free them to perceive the superior logic and validity of Christian truth. As stated by Robert E. Speer of the Student Volunteer Movement, the non-Christian religions are inadequate to meet the needs of men.

David continued to write, hour after hour, carefully explaining the details of the prospectus: the acquisition of suitable land, the buildings required, the number of faculty wanted and in which disciplines, the needs of a proper boarding department. He was a little hazy on some of these, since they had not yet pursued such a plan there in Adamu. He did have some information on the value of property and the cost of purpose-built structures.

He discussed the question of building permits and local hires. A charter to found the school would be issued in Pittsburgh and the school would be incorporated there. But they would still need to negotiate permissions not only with the Ottomans in Constantinople but with Buraan's own King, client of the Empire.

David filled page after page with the thick violet ink he had concocted, laying out each sheet on his desk, edges overlapping slightly, all of the writing exposed to the air. When the ink dried, it would have a blacker hue. But for now, he needed it to remain slightly damp, until the glycerin set just enough to make a pressure print. He carefully laid out the number of sheets of tissue he would need, and the right number of oiled sheets as well. Each sheet to be printed would have to be meticulously stacked, without smearing, under a sheet of tissue and a sheet of oiled paper. Once the stack was properly constructed, it would be placed into his letter-press, the iron slab lowered, and the screw tightened, just enough. It was a delicate process. But David had done it many times and had refined his technique.

However, it would be several hours before the ink reached the point of readiness, probably an hour or two after dawn. David was exhausted now from the intense effort of writing his best hand, on and on, without making the slightest mistake. He needed a bit of rest before starting the pressure print. If he slept for a few hours, he could come back early in the morning and finish the process.

He wearily climbed the stairs to his small apartment at the top of the Mission building. The fire in the grate had long since gone out. The sitting room and bedroom were cold and dark, but it scarcely mattered, since all he wanted to do was go to bed.

Before doing so, however, he knelt and laid before his Lord all of the cares of the day. Without earnest prayer, he would simply lie down and revisit all of the sins and errors he had committed all day long, while also worrying fruitlessly about the days to come.

Hidden in his bed, covered with a warm quilt stuffed with lamb's wool, he was quickly and deeply asleep.

When at last he woke, he was alarmed to discover broad daylight pouring through the windows. He had slept later than he intended, due to unusual fatigue. Dressing quickly, he headed downstairs to his office, hoping that he had not missed the proper moment when the glycerine ink was ready to print.

Chapter 2

Reaching his office door, he found to his surprise that it was not locked. He thought he had locked it as usual before retiring for the night. Opening the door, he stepped into near-darkness, as the wooden shutters over the windows were still firmly closed. Then, he became aware of a strange smell—partly metallic, partly animal. What on earth? There was also a quiet dripping sound. Incomprehensible.

Rushing to the windows, he unfastened the heavy shutters. Normally, Julius would do this before Galloway came downstairs. But Julius was away visiting his sister.

The shutters opened and light streamed into the room. His heavy oil lamp had been removed from its metal hook and bracket and was resting upon the floor. In its place, directly over the desk, was a very large haunch of meat, steadily dripping a watery trickle of blood onto the desktop.

David stared in shock at this bizarre arrangement. Who had done this? And why? With a glance he could see that most of the pages he had so carefully inscribed the night before were soaked, smeared, dissolved into a puddle of purple goo. Entirely ruined. The sheets of fresh tissue were also damp and scattered about, and some pages seemed to have bare footprints on them. And just to top it off, the small glass holding the remaining copying ink had been upset, and its contents had created a sticky purple blotch on the carpet under the desk.

He shook his head forcefully, repeatedly, as if he could reject this scene and somehow restore it to reason. "Julius!" he shouted, then remembered that the porter had gone and there was someone else on duty. Who was it? Bocksi.

"Bocksi?" he called down the hallway. "Bocksi! Are you there?"

After a few minutes, a skinny young fellow appeared, unperturbed. "*Ya mudeer!* Good morning."

"Ahhhhh, good morning to you, I'm sure. Can you please tell me what has happened in my office?"

The boy looked blank, standing in the hallway, calm and patient.

"Please, come inside, and tell me what this is." The boy's face brightened as they entered the office.

"Oh yes, *mudeer*, such a fine present! An entire beef quarter, a special gift to you, from Awadour the butcher. They slaughtered today just after dawn and he brought you the best part. The fattest calf, fine and fresh."

"Fresh, yes, extremely fresh," muttered Galloway. "Did you unlock my office for them? And why did they bring it here, instead of to the kitchen?"

"Oh yes, I used the keys of Julius, from the porter's room. They brought it here because it is a special present with the personal compliments of Mr. Awadour. Not just ordinary meat for the kitchen."

David's head was still spinning, as he added up the good intentions and innocent mistakes that had resulted in the loss of hours of careful work, and quite possibly a serious delay to the entire project. He needed to prepare a finished copy of the proposal before his international visitor arrived this week, in order to send it with her to the UPNA director in Pittsburgh. Could he get it done, again, before she arrived? Depending upon the unexpected interruptions and events of the next few days . . .

As he stood in the office thinking it through, a messenger arrived. David would need to leave at once for Kaskut.

Chapter 3

The sound of hammering on the door or the window shutters in the dark of night was nothing new for him. Someone's baby was coming fast, or someone was running a terrible fever or vomiting blood, or experiencing another urgent medical concern. As the only qualified physician in the American Mission and indeed the only one in central Buraan, Dr. Felix Marshall was permanently on call, as he had been for over forty years.

His feet hit the floor automatically and slid into his house-slippers. He donned his warm robe while walking toward the door.

A young child was waiting for him, a boy of about ten or twelve. The boy carried an oil lantern, as Buraani law required of anyone out after sundown. "Oh *duktoor*, sir," said the child, "Please come and help us. My brother has fallen into the fire and is burned. We are trying to help him but he is badly hurt." The child made this carefully-rehearsed announcement, then added in his natural voice, "Mama is very frightened."

Dr. Marshall spoke the Buraani language like his mother tongue.

"What time is it, do you know?"

"When I passed by the baker, he was in his shop." If the baker was at work, it was probably an hour or two before dawn.

"Come inside, child. Where have you come from?"

"From Faloun, sir."

"Faloun village? That's a long day's ride from here. Did you walk it somehow?"

"I got a ride part of the way, sir."

"Young man, I want you to lie down here on this sofa and rest, while I get ready. We shall leave at first light." The child was exhausted and in no condition for the return trip. Felix arranged him on the sofa with a pillow and a blanket and he was instantly asleep.

Unwilling to awaken his housekeeper, Felix went to the kitchen and lighted the gas ring. He brewed a pot of tea, and made a breakfast of bread and fig jam, looking in the cooler and the cupboards for eggs. He found three eggs in a bowl above the sink and boiled them briefly. He ate one of them, saving the other two for the boy.

After eating, Felix went back to his private room and sat at the desk. He began every day with an hour of Bible reading and prayer, offering up the day to come, remembering each of his friends, his colleagues, his patients. He prayed as usual for the McKinley family, then stopped abruptly as a wave of grief overtook him. Some time later he arose from the desk, got fully dressed, and carefully packed his medical bags with the supplies he was likely to need in this case.

Going out to the shed, he greeted his mule with a "Good morning, Polly," then made sure she had fresh water and some grain. Polly knew from long experience what was coming, so she availed herself of a nourishing breakfast and a stretch. Hauling feed and water for the mule was a chore normally done by others, and Felix found that it left him a bit winded, even light-headed. He braced himself against the stair rail and rested for a moment.

Felix saddled the mule and arranged the bags in the manner with which she was familiar. He knew her to be a creature of habit—diligent and faithful, but intolerant of surprises.

The first light of dawn was apparent now. Felix went into the house and woke the boy, then offered him bread, the two eggs, and a mug of hot tea. The child devoured them in a moment. "Time we were leaving," Felix said. He helped the boy climb up onto Polly's broad back and they set out.

As they passed the baker's shop, Felix stopped and bought several small round loaves, packing them into the saddlebags for later. It would take them most of the day to get to Faloun, even if they made only a few short halts.

It was, indeed, a very long day. Felix found that his legs continually cramped in an unusual manner, and he was forced to dismount and walk around until the pain and contortion ceased. There was also some tingling

Chapter 3

in his feet. After all, he was nearly 73 years old, so naturally long trips on a mule were less comfortable than in the past. They were climbing into the foothills of the Taurus Mountains and the path was rugged, with deep wadis or water-courses, now dry or with only a stream of snow-melt. Enough for Polly and themselves to have a drink.

As they approached Faloun village, the sun was low, but there was no need yet for the lantern. The boy directed him to a humble home on the edge of the village, where Felix was glad to dismount.

The child ran inside and brought out his mother, who tearfully expressed her thanks for his arrival. A little daughter of five or six was present as well, but she was sent immediately back inside by her mother to watch the patient. Everyone was introduced and exchanged routine blessings and expressions of concern. Felix quickly calculated that she was an abandoned spouse, since she spoke of a living husband but there was no sign of his presence; evidently she was left to bring up several children alone. He addressed her respectfully, using the honorifics for a married woman.

One of the few concessions Felix made to his advanced age was that he no longer required himself to memorize the name of every new person he encountered.

Following her into the house with his medical supplies, he at once saw the patient lying face down upon an improvised bed of carpets, beside the fire. In a Buraani home of this class, the hearth was merely an open fire pit, red with coals. A hood of sorts and a vent-hole carried most of the smoke out of the room. The fire was kept burning continually, since starting a new fire and reducing it to hot coals for cooking was a time-consuming task. If anyone was away from home for a few days and had to allow their fire to go out, they could go at dusk to fetch hot coals from the baker's shop, as he banked his fires at a low level during the hours of night.

He judged the boy on the bed of carpets to be about fourteen years of age—his mother's eldest son. He was clearly unconscious. Dr. Marshall's keen eye detected something in the position of the hands and arms—an awkwardness and rigidity—that suggested brain damage. Asking many specific questions, he determined that the child had suffered seizures from infancy, had serious motor disability, and cognitive impairments. The accident had occurred as the result of a seizure. While other members of the family were all engaged in work, the boy had dropped onto the hot coals of the fire and sustained serious burns on his back. The mother bitterly blamed herself for the accident. Felix tried to persuade her that seizures were unpredictable and accidents sometimes unavoidable, but without much success.

He asked for a place where he could wash, and was shown to the privy and hand-pump in the yard. Using carbolic soap, he scrubbed his hands thoroughly in the very cold water. "I shall need boiling water. Is the kettle ready?" he asked.

"In a moment, *duktoor*," she replied.

Bringing forth a graduated glass, he measured a pint of boiling water, then mixed in a heaping tablespoon of bicarbonate of soda. Leaving this to dissolve and cool, he placed all of his instruments in a small steel basin and poured boiling water on them to soak. While these lay cooling, he asked for a lantern, of which the family owned exactly one. The oil flame was not strong but some light was added by the cooking fire.

Felix made all of these preparations openly, in full view of the child's mother. He knew she could not trust anything that took place while she was unable to see what he was doing. He asked for her permission to examine the patient. She removed a blanket covering the boy's body and watched as Felix knelt beside him. He took the child's pulse, checked lymph nodes for signs of swelling, and opened his eyelids to judge the responsiveness of the pupils.

He was in a state of deep sedation. The mother had been treating him with a normal village remedy: poppy husks soaked in water to create an opiate solution. Opium poppies grew magnificently on the uplands in Buraan and represented the mainstay of the rural economy. She probably worked as a field hand during harvest season to support the family; part of the compensation for workers was the right to keep the empty husks after the putty-like secretions were scraped off and formed into small bricks of raw opium. The poppy water was commonly given to those suffering injuries or painful illnesses, laboring mothers, even restless children. It was keeping the boy quietly asleep.

Bracing himself for what he expected to find, Dr. Marshall began to remove the layers of cloth she had used to cover the injury. Some of the

Chapter 3

fibers had become stuck to the wound, and these he slowly softened and teased away using the soda solution and his sterilized instruments. When he finally got the injury field exposed, his worst fears were confirmed. The skin was entirely gone from large areas of the child's back. Not only that, but the underlying muscles were burned away as well, including those that support the spine, and bone was lying naked under his eyes. There was no treatment that could close such a wound. The child would not recover.

He carefully trimmed away all of the blackened tissue, and pierced blisters at one edge to allow serum to drain out. She observed every movement he made. When the wound was as prepared as he could make it, he brought out lengths of clean, soft cotton cloth from his bag, coated the wound lavishly with castor oil, and covered it with the fresh dressings. The entire procedure took about two hours. The little girl fell asleep on the rugs beside her mother.

As he came back to the fireside after washing again outdoors and lowered his tired body to the floor, she brought him a bowl of rice and lentils, with thick tomato sauce and a small onion. He prayed over it with sincere gratitude and consumed the hot food quickly, every last grain. "*Mamuji*, I thank you," he said using a term of affection common in families, meaning *little mother*. "Have you eaten?"

"Not yet."

"Please feed yourself and your children at once. Do not wait any longer." He knew that the custom of serving the guest—of serving the men—first was ironclad and must be observed.

"Thank you, *duktoor*."

Silence settled on the house while they ate, but it was an agitated silence. After the clearing up, Felix waited for her to speak, but she held back, shifting and moving her hands. At length he spoke.

"God is calling him, little mother," he said gently. "You know this, do you not?"

"Yes," she whispered, her face crumpling.

"Our Lord Jesus said, 'Let not your heart be troubled: you trust in God, trust also in me. In my Father's house are many homes, many rooms . . . I go ahead to prepare a place for you. I will receive you there.' God is gathering your child to himself, where he will find peace and relief from all suffering."

"But *duktoor* . . . why has my boy always been so ill? He has the falling sickness, and often gets hurt. He can't use his arms or hands, he can't speak . . . such a life, *duktoor*, for an innocent child."

Felix sighed deeply. What causes epilepsy? Or cerebral palsy? Science had no answer that he knew of. But she was not asking a question about medical science.

"Jesus also said: 'In this world you will have trouble; but take heart, for I have overcome the world.' We cannot understand many of the struggles of this life, especially why the innocent suffer. But Jesus himself was innocent, and he suffered pain and death at the hands of violent men. Yet he still loved, and he still trusted God, and God raised him from death to life."

The calling of a medical missionary was understood as a dual one: relieving physical suffering, while also extending spiritual aid as the opportunity arose. Felix never bothered to reflect on the theory or theology of missions. His desire to respond to human need of any kind came directly from the heart.

The coals glowed, the boy breathed quietly, and Felix waited. She did not ask any further questions, but he could see the tension slowly draining from her body, leaving only an immense weariness.

"*Mamuji*," he said. "I will watch the patient tonight. You and your daughter must go and rest. How long has it been since you slept in your bed?"

She blinked her eyes painfully. "Since the accident." At least three days.

"You must go now. If he needs anything, I shall do it."

"Thank you, *duktoor*. May your God bless you and fill you with peace."

"And you. Sleep well, *mamuji*."

She and the little girl went away into the inner room of the house, beyond the clattering curtain of carved wooden beads that separated the *salaamlek*, or reception rooms, from the *haraamlek*, or private family rooms, in every Buraani household, no matter how mean. This beaded curtain, the *katichess*, was an essential part of any marriage dower. So powerful was the privacy taboo that Felix knew she would relax and truly sleep only behind the curtain, and he hoped to restore her, physically and emotionally. He settled down to sit beside the patient on the woolen rugs and spend the night as he had at so many other bedsides in his long medical ministry.

Chapter 3

The hours passed. He tended the fire, napped a bit while sitting up, and communed in his heart with God. The young patient did stir at one point and wake just enough for Felix to give him a few swallows of the opium water. The boy sank back into his sedated sleep.

In the morning at first light, Felix went out to the latrine, then washed in the ice-cold water. He looked around for a bite of food but found none. From his saddlebags he retrieved a little bread and some dried apricots, which he chewed slowly beside the sleeping boy. The mother did not emerge from her bedroom.

A few hours later, she finally scrambled out from beyond the *katichess*, full of apologies for sleeping so late. She was keenly embarrassed at neglecting her guest, but Felix felt that his plan had succeeded, and she had accomplished a restorative night's sleep. She wanted to fix him breakfast but he needed to get on the road at once in order to be home by nightfall; he asked her to make him a cup of hot tea only.

"*Mamuji*, you should continue to keep the boy clean and quiet, and allow him to do as God commands. Can you do this?"

Her eyes were teary but she replied, "Yes, *duktoor*." The younger brother appeared from his place beyond the curtain, and Felix took him outside.

"My son, your mother will need you in the days to come. You must stay here and help her. Polly and I know the way home. There is no need for you to make the long journey again."

"But *duktoor*, you might not get through the pass before dark. At least take our lantern. Let me fill it with oil."

"No, child. If I incur a fine I shall pay it. Never mind." Felix knew how much it would cost the family to buy another lantern.

Summoning his own physical reserves, Felix saddled the mule and packed his things. He made a gentle farewell to the family and departed.

Massive dark clouds were speeding across the sky when he left and the air was laden with rain. Felix wrapped himself and his bags in his long oilcloth cloak and fastened the hood over his head. They made some hours' progress before the storm hit, pouring a lashing rain upon them. Very quickly, the narrow valleys filled with rushing water, and Polly's progress slowed. It was already late in the day when they approached the long pass. On the near side, a gully that had been dry a day ago was now a turbulent stream, and Polly struggled to get across it. The plateau ran with streaks of water. She picked her way around them and through the rocky upland from which all traces of a path had disappeared.

On the far side of the plateau, peering through the heavy rain, Felix saw with dismay that the fordable stream had become a wide, churning, impassable river. Polly stopped still and they both considered the situation. He urged her along the bank slowly in each direction, looking for a shallow or narrow spot where they might get across. There was none. At length he decided that they must return across the plateau and try to get back to Faloun village, pass another night there, and try again on the following day.

They clambered back through the rough upland. But when they reached the stream they had crossed earlier, it was too wild and swollen with water to get across it again. They were trapped upon the exposed plateau, without shelter, until the storm ended.

Felix checked his bags for any further food. He had packed very little and it was already gone. Polly could graze as needed, though she seemed too discouraged to do so. As darkness fell, they remained where they were. Felix saw that there was no way even to dismount, as nearly all the land around them that was not protruding rock was gushing water.

It was not the first time Dr. Marshall had spent a night in the saddle. He fastened a saddlebag strap around his body to prevent his falling upon the ground in his sleep, folded himself forward over Polly's neck, and tried to get some rest. Her body warmth helped to counteract the deep chill, and he was so exhausted by the demands of the past two days that he did spend much of the night in a wretchedly uncomfortable sleep.

When dawn broke, the rain had stopped, and there was hope that the water would recede. Felix woke with difficulty and tried to move. He found that his legs were entirely numb—a full paralysis. He then tried to unfasten the saddle strap holding his body on Polly's back, but his hands likewise would not obey him—they were stiff, cold, unresponsive. A sense of alarm seized him, and with it a sudden overwhelming pain in his side, like the thrust of a pitchfork. Pain and panic.

The pain speared up through his neck and into his shoulder, accompanied by a slap of nausea. He broke into a thick sweat despite the cold.

Chapter 3

After some moments of struggle, he understood what was happening, and a profound calm settled upon him. The pain subsided. He was able to inhale one last time and breathe out the word, "Father . . . " And then he was gone.

Polly stood indecisively on the plateau as the daylight increased, waiting for Felix to take some action. At last she stepped forward, munching a little forage that appeared as the water receded. She set off across the plateau toward home and encountered no objection from him; the slackened reins puzzled her but apparently that is what he wanted. When she reached the far side of the upland, the foaming river had dropped a great deal, and she found a shallow area where she could, with difficulty, ford across.

Polly arrived in Adamu at dusk, carrying the body of Felix Marshall. The first person in the town who recognized her and realized the meaning of her burden sent up a piercing wail of grief, bringing people running out of their houses. In moments, most of the neighbors were in the street, openly mourning the loss of their beloved doctor.

At length, someone thought to send word to David Galloway, and his week of stunning blows went on.

Chapter 4

The climb into the Taurus Mountains to Kaskut in March was no easy task, and under these circumstances, nearly unthinkable. David sent for the best horse in the Mission stables, a youngster with plenty of energy, to speed up the journey. Fortunately, he was a skillful rider. And he was familiar with the route from previous pastoral visits, conducted at more congenial times.

But David barely noticed the physical challenges of travel—he was unable to think about anything other than the brief but horrifying news of an attack on the village. The church destroyed, many dead. By this time, relatives of those lost would be converging upon Kaskut from other villages, trying to locate their loved ones, spiraling into a frenzy of grief.

Reverend McKinley itinerated among all of the Armenian Protestant congregations in the Maziret district. He was their pastor, too.

Missionaries in Buraan had some experience with these catastrophes. The Armenian communities of the Turkish Empire always existed on a knife's edge; the Ottoman government considered them to be alien to the authentic Turkish racial and cultural identity, and of very dubious sympathies. They were suspected of an inner allegiance to their Orthodox allies in Russia, and Russia never made any attempt to disguise its hostility toward the Turks and its designs on Turkish territory.

Armenians were also among those blamed for the 1908 revolt against Sultan Abdul Hamid II, since the new government proposed to extend fundamental legal rights to them. Many Turkish Muslims were adamant in rejecting Armenian equality on any terms.

Chapter 4

Only last year, they had faced a devastating attack on the town of Gorza, spreading through mob violence to Malatya, Hadjin, Marash and throughout the eastern province. In those dreadful incidents, Armenians were set upon by many of their Turkish neighbors, who resented the relative prosperity of the Armenian community and seized the chance to loot Armenian shops and homes. Assyrian and Greek Orthodox Christians were targeted as well.

Two young men, of the American Board of Commissioners for Foreign Missions, died in Gorza—shot while trying to fight an arson fire at the mission school for girls. Three female American teachers and the matron of the orphanage survived and provided harrowing eyewitness accounts of the violence to Western media.

David Galloway's own mission organization, the American Mission in Buraan, had not yet suffered directly from such attacks . . . until now.

When he reached Kaskut, he found a scene not of chaos, but of grimly controlled order. No one seemed particularly surprised by these events. Perhaps, after the Gorza region, they had assumed that their turn would come. Extended family and friends from nearby towns had sorted themselves into recovery and burial squads. Without time to construct proper coffins, they were committing the dead to the earth wrapped in blankets and bedsheets.

Under the pine trees, a thick carpet of fallen tags protected the earth from freezing. It was possible to scrape away the snow and pine needles to the bare ground beneath, then dig shallow graves. People were noting the location of their loved ones, with a view toward marking the graves or relocating the remains once they were reduced to bone. The practice of reinterring the dead was a very ancient one in the Near East and could be accepted when conditions demanded it.

But for their pastor, a proper burial was felt to be necessary. Simple coffins were created or brought in for Asa and Catherine. The tiny baby was nestled into Catherine's arms. These two coffins were left open for viewing and leave-taking, and held until Galloway's arrival. In the absence of flowers, people presented little green boughs from the trees, thin pencil-like candles, and bright bits of ribbon or strips of lace. It was a touching indication of what the McKinleys meant to them.

Asa's body was not charred by fire. It seemed that most of those in the church had died of smoke inhalation rather than burning. This made the task of identification easier.

David was hampered by his almost complete ignorance of the Armenian language. The people he encountered could communicate in Buraani for the most part. Gradually, he discovered the most appalling truth of this tragedy: several of the children were missing.

He had heard of the practice of raiders capturing children and trafficking them. The children were not kidnapped and returned to their families upon payment of ransom. They were taken away forever. Child labor was commonplace, and adding a worker in this manner could be easily concealed. With horror, David realized that two of the McKinley children were gone.

Carefully, he recorded the names of all of the children of Kaskut who were unaccounted for. It was not completely clear how many there were, but about twenty.

He asked a church elder from another congregation, who intended to stay and assist in the burials of the dead, to enumerate all of the persons found in the rubble of the church or lying somewhere in the compound, and to write down their names and family connections. It was evident that this would take some time.

The survivors requested that Reverend Galloway should bury their pastor with the formal Presbyterian order of worship. They asked him to use both English and Buraani, feeling that it was fitting to say goodbye to the McKinleys in their own native tongue. However, they stipulated that they wanted their kin to be buried using Armenian rites. They explained that an Armenian-speaking Presbyterian pastor had been sent for and would arrive in a few days to conduct their services.

David was aware that his ability to supply the pastoral needs of this population was limited. He supervised the closing of the coffins of Asa and Catherine . . . in the most frustrating detail of all, none of these people from outside of Kaskut could tell him what the baby's name was.

They had prepared two graves under the pines on the church grounds. Someone had even made grave markers, though they were written in

Chapter 4

Armenian script and David simply had to trust that the epitaphs were appropriate.

"Like as a father pitieth his children, so the Lord pitieth them that fear him. For he knoweth our frame; he remembereth that we are dust. As for man, his days are as grass; as a flower of the field, so he flourisheth. For the wind passeth over it, and it is gone, and the place thereof shall know it no more. But the mercy of the Lord is from everlasting to everlasting, and His righteousness unto our children's children."

He read the lengthy service as well as he could, translating it fluently into Buraani, struggling all the while to contain his own emotions.

"Oh Lord Jesus Christ, who thyself didst weep beside the grave, and art touched with the feeling of our sorrows: fulfill now thy promise that thou wilt not leave thy people comfortless, but wilt come to them. Reveal thyself unto thine afflicted servants, and cause them to hear thee saying, 'I am the Resurrection and the Life.' Help them, O Lord, to turn to thee with true discernment, and abide in thee through living faith; that, finding now the comfort of thy presence, they may have also a sure confidence in thee for all that is to come, until the day break, and these shadows flee away. Hear us for thy great mercy's sake, O Jesus Christ Our Lord. Amen."

David completed the liturgy, and then he did something that the assembled people did not expect: he began to sing. He was a trained church-choir tenor with a fine voice, and gospel music had always been vitally important to him, from earliest childhood. Growing up in Lexington, Virginia, he was surrounded by traditional American folk music, Sacred Harp singing, and the expert instrumentalists of the Shenandoah Valley. His ability had been refined as a student at the Union Theological Seminary in Virginia, and he understood the power of music to touch the spirit. He had taught his congregation in Adamu many of the simple, lovely songs of his youth, easily translated into Buraani, easily amplified by improvisation.

"There are angels hovering round . . . there are angels hovering round . . . there are angels, angels hovering round."

The faces of the people softened.

"Your people are coming home . . . your people are coming home . . . your people, Lord, your sons and daughters are coming home."

Even those who did not understand Buraani were drawn in. Tears appeared on many faces.

"Oh Jesus, we trust in you . . . Oh Jesus, we trust in you . . . Oh Jesus, Jesus we trust in you." At his point they began to sing with him, and the slow, sweet melody quickly developed into harmony.

"Have mercy on us, Lord . . . have mercy on us, Lord . . . have mercy, mercy on us, Lord."

The people had instinctively moved closer together, and now many were embracing with tears. He had been able to do that for them, at least—he had validated their repressed emotion and allowed them to grieve together.

Galloway stayed that night at the empty manse, and went carefully through the McKinleys' papers and personal effects. The pillagers had taken mainly items like jewelry and coin. He packaged up their important documents, correspondence, and photographs, intending to take them back to Adamu and send them on to their family in Ohio.

In the morning, he began the return trip. The temperature was rising a little and he encountered a lot of melting snow, but still made good time down from the mountains.

Back in his office, he found that his desk had been cleaned up somewhat, and only hoped that none of the papers he still needed had been thrown away. He drafted a cable to the American Embassy in Constantinople, explaining what had happened, appealing for assistance, and naming each of the missing children. He knew that there was little point in reporting the incident to the palace at Dameotis. Buraan's ruler was a king in name only, subject to his Ottoman overlords at the Sublime Porte. He prepared another cable, anyway.

Julius was still out of town and David was not about to entrust a task like this to Bocksi or another helper, so he went to the regional telegraph station himself.

When he returned, waiting for him was a written message from Louisa Booth, the American Mission's superintendent of primary schools. She normally resided in Osmaneyya but happened to be in Adamu and wished to see him. It was more than a message—a summons, really. He prepared himself and went out again, to the girls' school where Miss Booth stayed when she was in town.

Chapter 4

He found her at the office of the principal, where she had ensconced herself. The principal stood awkwardly beside the desk until she was dismissed.

"Reverend Galloway, thank you for coming here. I felt we needed to discuss the events of recent days." He felt like a miscreant student called to the principal's office.

"The events of recent days have been tragic in the extreme. I have just returned from Kaskut."

"Tragic, indeed. Another outrageous crime against American missionaries in this country. I shall never understand how these people come to believe that they have any right to behave in such a manner. It must not be tolerated."

David regarded Miss Booth warily. She sat rigidly in her seat, wearing a Victorian dress that had been the norm a generation ago, when she first arrived in Buraan. He was waiting for her to observe, again, that she had been serving in the mission field nearly since he was born, with more than thirty years of experience. She was now sixty and considered herself an authority on all aspects of local life and work. Galloway was relatively young for a head of mission—only thirty-eight, now—but he was ordained and had both a university and a graduate seminary education. And twelve years of experience in the field.

"The American Embassy in Constantinople has been notified. I expect they will make a formal complaint to the Porte and request their assistance, in apprehending the attackers, and in locating the missing children." David wanted to kick himself—the news had just slipped out. But it would soon become common knowledge in any case.

"The missing children? Whatever do you mean?"

"There were many dead—still recovering the bodies, so I am not sure precisely how many. But also, about a score of children were abducted, evidently."

She drew herself up, ready to fly into a fury. "Why, that is utterly unacceptable! Please don't tell me the McKinley children were among them."

"I regret very much to report that the two eldest children, Anne and Matthew, have not been found."

"Well, surely, this is not a matter to be left to those heathen at the Porte! We must demand that the American military be mobilized."

"Nobody has the authority to deploy the U.S. Army. Not even the Embassy."

"So, we merely file a complaint, and leave it at that?"

"We have no choice. There is no application of force that could rectify this, even if we had the power to exert it."

"Mr. Galloway, I must say that I find your response to be entirely inadequate." He hated it when she called him that, instead of Reverend Galloway. It seemed to be a deliberate attempt to belittle his pastoral leadership.

"Inadequate or not, there it is."

"I repeat, unacceptable! We simply cannot allow the arrogance of the late-called races to go unchallenged. Their effrontery will know no bounds. We are appointed to be the Lord's weapons of righteousness, and we must take up arms against this foe!"

"What? Weapons of righteousness?"

"Romans, chapter six, verse thirteen. We are to present ourselves to God as weapons of his righteousness. I have only just prepared a Sunday School lesson on this passage."

David too knew the passage well. "Actually, that word—it's *hopla* in the Greek—it's normally translated as instruments or tools, not weapons."

"The Apostle Paul did not hesitate to use military figures in his writing—the full armor of God, the helmet of salvation, the sword of the Spirit. It is not our role to be timid and passive."

"If we are discussing the book of Romans, we should then refer to chapter thirteen, where Paul instructs us to be subject to the governing authorities. As John Calvin confirmed, temporal rulers are established by God and we are required to submit to them. Even those who are viewed as unfit or unjust."

"Oh, well, that's just sheer nonsense."

"Not at all, Miss Booth. In the last chapter of the *Institutes*, Calvin presents a closely-reasoned argument for the divine appointment of earthly rulers and the proper use of civil law to maintain order."

"Maintain order? The Turks did a very fine job of maintaining order in Kaskut, did they not? And in Gorza, Hadjin and Marash? Surely Calvin

Chapter 4

did not intend that citizens of advanced and Christian nations should be subject to Mohammedan despots. That's simply degrading, and absurd."

"Jesus himself submitted to the pagan Roman occupiers," said David, in a softer voice. "He acknowledged the Roman Empire and its rights, and even accepted its cruel and unjust punishments, unto his own agonizing death."

There was a pause, as Louisa Booth's indignation stalled against the example of the Lord Jesus himself. Galloway could have upheld both sides of this argument. The evidence from Scripture was inconclusive, as it appeared that at times God commanded his people to take up literal weapons in battle. Many of the great heroes of old were warriors, such as Joshua, Gideon, David and Saul. And even in the New Testament, echoes of warfare were heard, in language used for spiritual struggle and conflict. It was not a straightforward issue by any means.

"On a purely practical level, I see no other options," David said. "We can't identify the attackers, and we have no idea where they have gone. No way to trace the children. The raiders will dispose of them to willing buyers, who will put them to work weaving carpets or cleaning floors, and intimidate them into silence. How could anyone find them?"

"Do the Armenians have ties with other communities, where they might hear of some information?"

"This is one possibility, and I have asked them to let us know at once if anything is learned about any of them. Not clear how realistic this is. I declare to you, if I could come up with any other course of action, you may be sure that I would pursue it."

"What about the McKinleys' family at home?"

"I went through their belongings in Kaskut, and there were some photographs and papers I thought they might wish to have. I will write to their parents as soon as I have a chance." He inhaled slowly and sighed. "All of us knew when we accepted God's call to the mission field that we would face years of absence from our loved ones, the risk of violence, accidents, illness, and loss. We have buried those nearest and dearest to us. We have endured separation from everything we value at home. But in this, too, we only follow the Lord in our small way."

As David sat thinking, his irritation and combativeness faded away. It was not within his deepest nature to be combative, even in the face of provocation.

"Blessed are they that mourn, for they shall be comforted," David recited quietly. "Blessed are the merciful, for they shall obtain mercy. Blessed are they which are persecuted, for theirs is the Kingdom of Heaven."

Louisa Booth seemed to have lost her desire to prove her point. Underneath her demanding tone, she was sad and scared. She loved the McKinleys as well, especially their children. And she did fear the rising tide of anti-Christian violence around them, as bad as anything she had seen since the Hamidian pogroms in the 1890s. She simply sat and listened.

"You have heard that it was said, 'An eye for an eye, and a tooth for a tooth.' But I say to you, resist not evil; but whosoever shall smite you on your right cheek, to him turn the other also."

David continued, "You have heard that it was said, 'Love your neighbor, and hate your enemy.' But I say to you, love your enemies, bless them that curse you, do good to them that hate you, and pray for them that despitefully use you and persecute you . . . that you may be children of your Father, which is in heaven."

There was no way back from these words of Jesus, no ambiguity to negotiate with. David's stress and fatigue were making themselves felt, and he thought it was evident that no operational plan was about to emerge from his discussion with Louisa.

"Miss Booth," he said, "Seeing as how you are here in Adamu, is there anything you need for the Mission schools? Have you any report or requests to make?"

"I think not," she replied. "We are teaching and learning on a normal basis, and no extraordinary expenses are anticipated. There is anxiety among the Armenian students and teachers, of course. We shall do what we can to address it."

"Thank you. I know we can rely upon your leadership."

"I shall conduct routine visits and inspections among the four schools in town," she continued. "I need to stop at several other towns and villages on my way back to Osmaneyya. I am concerned about the boarding school

Chapter 4

at Ypli Dag, because I believe there are some Armenian boys there who come from Kaskut, or nearby villages. They may need support."

"Very good. If you need any assistance with that, please send word. And by the way, we are expecting an American visitor tomorrow, just passing through on her way to Europe and the United States. So if you have any letters you would like her to post, you may give them to me."

"There are some—in my room. If you can wait for a few minutes I'll go and get them."

"Yes, do. I'll wait."

Miss Booth got up quickly and hurried out. David sat still with his eyes closed and listened for her return. When she opened the door of the office, he stood up respectfully and accepted the letters. Hand-carried mail was rarely intercepted by the Ottoman border officials and stood a good chance of reaching its destination, unlike letters sent through the Turkish post.

He held out his hand to her. "Thank you for this conversation," he said. "I do appreciate it. Your wisdom and experience are unmatched."

"The honor is mine," she said, disarmed. "Thank you for your leadership of the Mission at this difficult time."

"Pray for us," he said.

"Of course. I assure you, I do."

"God bless you, Miss Booth. If you will excuse me."

There were clouds gathering in the west, signs of a heavy rain on the way. David decided he had just enough time to go along to the Presbyterian church to see if there were any problems or messages that required his attention, having been out of town. In fact, the moment he walked through the door the porter asked to speak to him.

It took about two hours to deal with those institutional issues. And when he left to walk back to the Mission building, the sky was black and pelting rain.

Chapter 5

David Galloway had another hurdle to face—the planned visit of Suzanna Hardy, the wife of John Campbell Hardy, one of Pittsburgh's leading steel manufacturers and the principal donor to the American Mission in Buraan. Pittsburgh lay in the heart of UPNA country—the United Presbyterian Church of North America—from which all of the AMB staff were sent and supported.

Mrs. Hardy loved to travel and was inherently interested in everything. The elite social circle in Pittsburgh quickly bored her, so she spent large blocks of time investigating the worldwide deployment of Mr. Hardy's charitable giving. She was much younger than her husband, who seemed to accept that the price of having a delightful, effervescent, intelligent, glamorous wife was allowing her enough freedom to enjoy herself.

Galloway was at the AMB offices early to wait for her. His heart sank to think of the spoiled proposal for a new Mission college in Buraan, which he had intended to place in her hands today for personal delivery to the UPNA in Pittsburgh. The missed deadline could mean many months of delay in the initiation of the project. Perhaps longer, unless he could find another way to convey the document.

In midmorning came the *hantour* or horse-drawn coach from the only presentable hotel in Adamu.

"My dear Mrs. Hardy, such a pleasure to see you! Let me offer you the heartiest welcome, from the whole of the American Mission."

"Reverend Galloway, wonderful to see you again! I do so enjoy coming here. And how convenient, here you are on the way between Cairo and Paris . . . at least, by a somewhat circuitous route."

Chapter 5

"I didn't realize that you were in Egypt. I thought you were arriving here from Crete."

"Well, you know, I used to come out every spring and work with Harriet Boyd—that is, now Harriet Hawes—at her dig site in Crete. What fun we had camping in the mountains and digging up that ancient business! It was like a girls' club or a sorority trip, just out there with Harriet, and that girlfriend of hers, Edith Hall, and Blanche What's-her-name before that, and about a hundred Greek men." David's face reminded her that he wasn't always prepared for her jocular tone.

"Harriet couldn't come back to Gournia this season, seeing as how she just had a baby. But that's all right, it enabled me to spend several weeks in Egypt at Luxor and Aswan instead, which are perfectly fascinating, and beautiful this time of year. Saw all of the work done by Flinders Petrie, and met that ambitious student of his, Howard Carter. I learned that Carter doesn't require a patron at the moment, since he's now under the wing of Lord Carnarvon, so instead of doing dig work, I just spent time visiting everything and having drinks on the terrace of the Old Cataract Hotel. I do know how to relax and simply enjoy myself, when the occasion arises."

"Glad to hear that you had such a pleasant stay."

"Oh yes, it was wonderful, apart from the normal vexations of life in Egypt, which simply add to the experience, in my view. Gordon did everything he could to keep me safe and comfortable, as he always does, so I have nothing to complain about. You would love Egypt, I'm sure of it. You must come with me some time." David knew that Mr. Gordon was Mrs. Hardy's factotum and protector on all of her journeys, along with Odine, her lady's maid. He doubted that they encountered any hardship that she did not undertake voluntarily, simply for the adventure of it.

"So, I brought you a few things, in this magic bag," she said, indicating the large satchel by her side. "Do let us go sit in this lovely mild sunshine. Can we have a couple of chairs brought out?"

David had a word with someone in the hallway and suitable accommodation was made. He did find Suzanna Hardy a bit difficult to keep up with, at times. She was so adapted to social life at a rarefied level, conversations of sparkling wit, knowing everyone worthy of attention, and going anywhere she pleased. He had to make an effort just to plod along with her, and in his weakened state, he was not equal to it.

"Ah yes, this is just the thing. In Egypt one must take care not to be exposed to the direct sun, even in the winter or early spring. It's liable to make one groggy, or worse. How pleasant to feel this warmth on one's face! So straightaway, let me give you one of the things I've brought."

From her bag, she produced a book wrapped in brown paper to keep it clean. Inside he found the coveted third volume of James Dennis' *Christian Missions and Social Progress*, published in 1906. "Oh, but this is exactly what I've been waiting for!" David exclaimed. "The first two volumes were so impressive. I didn't dare ask anyone to use their precious freight allotment to bring me books."

"Well of course you wanted it. Didn't you talk endlessly about Dennis the last time I was here? About missions as the ideal dynamic power in the advancement of societies all round the world, molding and uplifting public affairs, serving commercial expansion, stimulating the moral and religious improvement not only of individuals but of nations as a whole? You see, not only did I listen to you, but I read bits of it myself on the long voyage over here." She was very pleased with herself.

"I can't thank you enough," he said.

"You must remember that I don't travel with a freight allotment, but with steamer trunks filled with party frocks and silver tea sets and silk sheets. Mr. Gordon sees to that. That is, Odine packs them and Gordon makes sure they come along with us. It's a ridiculous luxury, to be sure. But I have plenty of room for a few books."

"I appreciate it very much, truly. In particular, that you remembered our earlier conversations."

"Reverend Galloway, I think you underestimate my sincere interest in the American Mission here. It's not all tea on the terrace, I understand that. Your work is of the utmost importance in the service of God's Kingdom, and it's my privilege to assist in little ways."

Her sudden seriousness brought him up short, and somehow closed his throat with emotion. At a time when he doubted the whole point of the Mission itself, and the unspeakably high cost of it in lives and suffering, her faith struck him hard.

Chapter 5

"I have been told about your terrible losses . . . the McKinley family . . . such a horror. I can scarcely believe it. And then Dr. Marshall as well. You must be reeling. I am so very, very sorry."

David was unable to form a single word. Vivid images of Asa and Catherine and their little children rushed into his mind, and Felix was as real as if he had been sitting with them at that moment. And then, unbidden, came other intense memories. Of his own wife, Mary Dale, and their dear daughter Anne.

It was six years ago that he was attending the regional meeting of American Mission senior staff in Beirut, when cholera swept through the countryside, as often happened in the summertime. Beirut was placed under military blockade, no one allowed in or out. David was frantic to return to Adamu but was unable to leave. It was eleven long days before he found someone who was susceptible to persuasion, in a position to look the other way while he escaped. Then, travel through Syria and Buraan was impeded at every turn, with armed patrols, besieged towns with empty streets, near-total lack of food and other provisions, attacks by bandits who tried to steal his horse and any other valuables. It was a desperate journey.

When he finally reached home, a more desperate scene awaited him. Mary Dale was already dead, and their precious child lay wasting quickly. He learned from those caring for her that when his wife was first struck with the illness, she sent all of the Buraani Christians away—the cook and housekeeper, other helpers—to prevent them being infected as well. They returned every day to try to help her, but she sent them away again and again, as she struggled to care for herself and Anne alone.

When she was too weak and dehydrated to stand, she was still attempting to wash their soiled sheets and bedclothes, when she apparently lost consciousness and fell, striking her forehead against the edge of the enameled iron sink. She probably died from the blow. The next day, when her faithful friends returned, Mary Dale did not come to the door and stop them. They entered and found her body, and the child barely living.

David had brought back from Beirut a little of the Hamlin Cholera Remedy—equal parts laudanum, camphor and rhubarb—and he made an effort to treat the child with it. Her poor face was shrunken, eyes bulging in deep sockets, her pretty hands reduced to bone and wrinkled skin. It was impossible to save her. She died there before his eyes. His lovely Anne, only seven years old. Like the McKinley daughter, also called Anne, also seven years old. This freakish coincidence was haunting his heart. The two girls had merged in his mind in a way that confused and tormented him.

"I can do nothing—nothing to save her. To save them."

"I shall send word to the Embassy in Constantinople. Perhaps we can put pressure on them in some way to search for the captured children. Buy them back, even. Something!"

"We have informed them . . . surely they will not allow Americans to be abused in this fashion, if there is anything to be done. Not confident they will intervene for the rest of the children, the Armenians. There is hope that the Armenian community itself can use its contacts to locate them . . . though we have no idea where they have been taken, and the Turkish government is unlikely to be of any use. From the point of view of the Porte, another Armenian village destroyed is of negligible concern. But the disappearance of the McKinley children might be a greater political quandary for them."

"I should think so, too. Such a nightmare! How many dead?"

"I don't even know, exactly. I went up to bury Asa and Catherine and their baby, but I don't speak Armenian, and they wanted those funeral services in their own language. Asa, of course, was their pastor, and the only ordained American Mission member here who ministered in Armenian. They asked the Mission to send someone from Beirut." Useless again. Unable to help.

"Tell me about Dr. Marshall."

"Felix was the most devoted, selfless missionary physician anyone could ask for. I've known many in various places, and they tend to be of that nature. But Felix was the very soul of benevolence. He was my most trusted friend."

"I am at a loss. I don't know what to tell you, except how sorry I feel."

"I know. Words fail at such a time."

He fell silent as the extent of his loneliness stretched out before him. Without a wife, without a child, without a colleague, without a friend. Some workers seemed to function well when deprived of human connections, but David was not one of them.

Chapter 5

The life of the town somehow went on around them. They could hear *hantours* passing in the street outside, cats wailing, people shouting, doors and windows slamming, donkeys braying, children squealing and yelling at one another. Adamu was normally a very noisy place. If Buraanis practiced tranquil introspection, they apparently did it somewhere else.

The early spring sunshine, of barely perceptible warmth, filled the small courtyard. Her soft amber hair was gathered loosely around her face and gleamed golden in the light. She was wearing a fashionable chiffon tea dress, butter yellow with a print of tiny green sprigs, lace around the open square neckline and elbow-length sleeves. A green silk sash around the waist—and clearly, no corset. It revealed only a little of the skin one would see with an evening gown, but it was enough.

David perceived none of these details, only a glowing blur of sunny color, in the most graceful feminine shape. His mind absorbed the impression and began to envision seeing through the clothing, images of her rounded bosom and belly, her pearly thighs, her hidden depths. Certainly not thoughts he should be having about another man's wife.

He emitted a strangled sound like a groan of pain, then covered it quickly with a cough, then more coughs. Startled, she saw that he was in distress, and assumed it was another moment of grief.

"Sorry," he croaked. "The dust . . . "

"Oh, I was just thinking that the air here is so delightfully clear and fresh, not at all like Egypt. Oh my, the filth and the dust! People imagine that a desert sandstorm throws up grains from the dunes, like beach sand. But over the Libyan desert what towers up in great roiling clouds is not sand, but a very fine pulverized rock, like classroom chalk powder. Absolutely chokes you and drives itself into every crevice. Darkens the sky like nightfall, often with an infernal reddish glow. I declare, I had no appreciation for the plagues of Exodus before going through a proper Cairene dust-storm. Or sleeping in certain Egyptian hotel beds, as well."

As she chatted on she watched him carefully. He was an inch away from an irretrievable emotional breakdown, which she knew would humiliate him. He was still lodged in Victorian times in many ways, as much as old Miss Booth. She continued to give him time to regain his composure.

"I beg your pardon, Mrs. Hardy . . . "

"Please," she said gently. "We have been friends for years. Please call me Suzanna. And in my mind, you are David and you always have been." A ripple of intimacy passed between them.

"David, you are going through a kind of personal perdition right now. We both know that. You have suffered an overwhelming loss, several of them, in fact. You need to be compassionate with yourself, just as you would be with any other person who is shaken and grieving. Now listen, I sound like *your* pastor," she added with a smile. "Often it's harder for those who lead a community and feel that they must stay strong, for the sake of the others. Well . . . I regret to inform you that you are human, too."

He smiled a little at this, for the first time in many days. "I'm so thankful that you are here," he whispered.

"You will be even more thankful when I show you the rest of the gifts I brought you." Rummaging through her bag, she brought out a bundle wrapped in cloth. "This I brought with the permission of dear Harriet. Go ahead, open it."

Inside several layers, he found a small clay vessel, with a tiny mouth and broad shoulders. It was a cocoa color overall, but painted on its molded curves in a sinuous lifelike pose was a strange sea creature, perhaps an octopus or squid, with vigorous black tentacles wrapping round, and wide staring eyes.

"Mycenaean of course, from the Vasiliki site, about two miles southeast of Gournia. It's not what is coming to be known as Vasiliki ware—I found those rather ugly, to be honest. This comes from an upper level, perhaps Minoan Two. Charming little squid or something, isn't it? They found two hundred baskets full of pottery fragments there, upon my word. This wasn't quite intact, but Harriet's assistant Aristedes is a perfect genius at reconstructing the pottery—you can't even see where he has glued it together. Isn't it just a pip?"

"Suzanna, such a delight! I never thought to possess such a thing. Thank you so very much."

"Oh my pleasure, I'm sure. Think of me earning that artifact by sleeping in a drafty tent on a pile of straw, and you will have a sense of my esteem for you."

"A costly gift."

Chapter 5

"I think so! Not to mention having to listen to Edith's constant prattle for six weeks . . . I tell you, that woman simply could not shut her mouth." Suzanna's hazel eyes were alight, as she skillfully raised his spirits with her charm. She was very fond of this diligent, well-intentioned, idealistic man, and looked forward to her visits there. Like many strong and capable women, she liked being in a position to help men when they faltered . . . it was partly ego, yes, but also a natural desire to set things right.

"And now you must look at this. It's my special gift to you, requiring much cooperation from a number of people. Another reason why I would love to take you with me to Egypt. But barring that, this will have to be the next best thing."

There was a bound volume—a photograph album—and a folder full of loose papers. In the folder he found a printed leaflet headed *Assiut College, American Mission in Egypt*, and what seemed to be sheets of correspondence. The leaflet was a detailed description of the College: its faculty and staff, enrollment, curriculum, expenses, means of support, physical facilities, everything. The correspondence included testimonials of appreciation for the college, from such sources as the United States Ambassador to Egypt, professors at Yale, Union Theological Seminary in Virginia, Princeton and McCormick Seminary in Chicago, the Anglican Bishop of Egypt and the Sudan, the Moderator of the Synod of the Nile, heads of the American Bible Society and Christian Endeavor . . . and such missionary statesmen as John R. Mott and Samuel Zwemer, in whose company David could only imagine himself.

He opened the photo album. Inside were scores of photos of Assiut College buildings and people, often with Mrs. Hardy standing beside them. The photos were artfully affixed on the pages with captions identifying everyone and everything. She moved close beside him as he leafed through the book, pointing out certain things and telling him little details about the scenes he was looking at. She was reveling in his openmouthed reaction.

"So there, you see? It's almost like being there yourself. Found a good photographer in Cairo and brought him along with us. I got them to record every bit that might be useful to you. Isn't it inspiring? We *can* do this, you see. They did it right there, in that poky little town in Upper Egypt, and we can do it here, in Adamu."

"It's . . . it's perfectly marvelous, Suzanna. All of this information—it will be *so* helpful as we try to plan and build our new school. I am . . . simply in awe. So much care and thought went into this . . . again I am entirely in your debt."

"Oh gracious, it was such fun! Of course, the American Mission in Egypt is UPNA as well, so Mr. Hardy and I have been involved there for some time, and we help to support Assiut College. But I had never been there before. Such an attractive campus, well laid out, well built. Hundreds of irresistible children! Apart from the unbearable climate eight months of the year, it's just a wonderful place."

"Well, they have a forty-year head start on us, after all."

"Indeed they have, but just wait and see us catch up, and perhaps surpass them."

"Listen to this, Suzanna, in the pamphlet here: 'In 1865 Assiut College was started as a day school in a renovated donkey stable . . . five boys were present on the first day, and the total enrollment of the first year was about twenty.' We've got that right now, have we not? Only we are meeting in a cellar rather than a stable. The boys call us 'Cellar College,' and that's about right."

"One must begin somewhere! The mustard seed grows into a mighty tree. From the acorn comes the oak. Like that."

His face fell as he took a long, slow breath. "I have nothing for you, Suzanna. Not even the prospectus to deliver. I wrote it out for you to take today, and the paper was destroyed. An accident. No gifts, no plan, nothing. I have failed."

"I hate to hear you talk like that. I mean, it's not your fault these things have happened. It's a monstrous great mass of setbacks, yes, but it has come upon us like the desert dust-storms. We just need to wait for it to pass, then clean up the mess and carry on. Isn't that so?"

He sat there trying to gather his wits. They were sitting so close together to look through the photo album that his arm and hers were nearly touching. The sunshine was causing a sweet, vaguely floral scent to rise from her hair or her skin . . . probably some expensive French soap or lotion, or a Provençal perfume. Or perhaps it was the scent of the woman herself.

Chapter 5

"I tried to find time to write it out again, but I could not. It will just have to wait until another traveler comes through."

"No, just a minute there . . . I have an idea. Now let's see, this is the seventeenth . . . where is my date book? Yes, here it is." She found a tiny journal in her bag and turned to the right spot. "Now, I am scheduled to leave for Athens tomorrow, to board the ship bound for Paris. I believe it's three weeks in Paris, then the voyage across the Atlantic. However . . . none of these dates were handed down on Mount Sinai, now were they? Let me have a little talk with Mr. Gordon, he's so good at this."

He began to see where her thoughts were going. "Do you mean, if your plans can—"

"Oh, I have no doubt that our plans can be changed. Suppose I were to stay in Buraan for another week, would that be long enough? Surely there are plenty of small boats going between Dameotis and Athens, or Piraeus actually. Even ones with no passenger accommodation rarely present a problem. The captain is almost always ready to give up his cabin to a guest who makes it worth his while. And the major shipping lines are seldom unable to find a first-class stateroom for a frequent passenger. It will be a matter of a few telegrams from Dameotis to the P&O, I should think. My friend, there is no problem here that cannot be solved by the judicious application of resources."

He stared at her, again in awe. She was ready for anything.

"So, tell me if this will work. Can you prepare a new prospectus in a few days? Perhaps you could use some of this information I brought from Assiut College to make it an even stronger proposal. Perhaps—"

"Oh of course, that's brilliant. There is excellent detail here—I can rewrite the proposal. Some of it was poorly constructed the first time, because I didn't have realistic estimates of the staffing and expenses. This will help enormously." He began to feel alive again. "I have some commitments in the next few days—a pastoral visit to Peshtaran tomorrow, and then service for the Lord's Day. But I could work on it beginning on Monday and give it a fresh start."

"That's the spirit, my dear. You know we can get it done."

Again he paused. "I don't know what to do, though, about the local board of management. Asa and Felix, they were central to this plan."

She thought for a moment. "If I may, I have a suggestion. Use their names as you intended. I can explain the situation to John and to Mr. Casters when I see them . . . we will just have to recruit men to take their places."

"All right, I'll do that. Also . . . there is a packet of personal belongings to send to the McKinleys' parents. Felix had no one left at home, after all these years."

"Of course, I shall take it and see to it that it is delivered. You get busy and write up that proposal. I'll use a few days here to write letters I've been meaning to get to, and I think I'll visit all of the Mission schools for little ones, especially the girls. Yes, that will be lovely."

"Suzanna, you have given me back my heart."

"In fact, I can plainly see that," she teased a bit, smiling. "Just one of my many talents, if I do say so myself. I have the ability to draw others out of the slough of despond."

"You do. That you do."

"If we are to accomplish our aims, I must speak to Mr. Gordon at once. He will have complicated arrangements to make."

"Of course."

"And I would venture to guess that you also haven't had a decent meal in long time. Very important for the morale, you know. I want you to come with me to the hotel for lunch. I can't say that their restaurant is the best I've ever tried, but it's serviceable; I had a decent dinner last night. So please, come with me, and let's try fortifying the body as well as the soul."

"Thank you. Again."

She also knew when to stop chatting, and simply gave him a long, knowing look, one that nearly sucked the breath out of his body. He simply would never consider any trespass with her, and he felt sure that she would reject such an idea as well. But he could love her just the same, with a chaste and ardent love, and take strength from her presence.

The *hantour* was still waiting in front of the American Mission building, and they climbed in together, setting off for the hotel.

Chapter 6

One reason why things were not under control at the Presbyterian church in Adamu during David's absence was that his pastoral assistant had also gone out of town. Shueyda Momonen was bright, capable, and entirely dedicated to his faith and work. But David also found him unpredictable, and somewhat mysterious.

Shueyda was the product of a Christian family, among the early adopters of the faith. His father was a quiet, thoughtful man, a deep reader, who had become interested in the scholarly preaching of Presbyterian missionaries and discovered his place in that community. His mother likewise immersed herself in her Christian life. It was she who raised Shueyda to love worship and prayer, and especially the growing corpus of Buraani-language songs that related Bible stories and expressed devotion.

They sent their son to the American Mission primary school for boys. Had there been a secondary school or college, he would have continued. In the event, he studied on a sort of apprenticeship or tutorial basis with David Galloway, and was one of the most promising graduates of the "Cellar College."

But when Shueyda was still an adolescent, something happened in his spiritual life. It was a kind of radicalization. He somehow transformed from a diligent follower into a leader; he acquired a new strength and a commitment to share the Gospel with those who were outside the comfortable Christian community in which he had been raised.

Shueyda began to talk to others about his faith—not in an aggressive manner, but selectively. He seemed to sense it when a person was ready to be approached, and with a gentle question or two, opened a dialogue that often resulted in that person spilling forth inner conflicts and longings that Jesus was standing by to deal with.

Soon, Shueyda was going out on one-man mission expeditions of his own, on a sturdy old black bicycle, bringing a little food, a Bible and a clean shirt in a bag hanging from the handlebars. He would go to a town or village where no church existed and begin getting to know people. He also looked for ways to be of assistance, helping someone load melons onto a donkey cart, or pump water from the village well. On occasion, he would preach openly, but more often he would seek personal conversations with individuals, or approach groups of men resting in the shade of a tree, or women washing clothes in the river. On Sundays he would sing Christian songs and teach a simple Bible lesson to anyone who stood or sat nearby long enough to hear it.

He was not as good at carrying out the routine administrative tasks of serving a church in a pastoral role. It frustrated David to have Shueyda disappear on one of his mission trips and be away for an unknown period of time, when there was work to be done in looking after the Adamu congregation. When David would challenge him on this, Shueyda simply replied, "I am an evangelist." It was a statement of fact, like "I am twenty-one years old." The expectation was that David would obviously accept this. It seemed at times to David that Shueyda was training him, instead of the other way round.

David remembered the last time Miss Booth had been in Adamu for her regular inspection of the local Mission schools, about a year ago. That was another occasion when a summons had come to him at the AMB offices from Miss Booth, requiring him to visit her at once at the boys' school. It was a Monday morning, when David cherished a few hours of quiet after his demanding Sunday. But no.

When Galloway arrived, he found Miss Booth and the headmaster conferring in the hallway, while sounds of boisterous childhood emerged from a classroom. Miss Booth turned to him with her face an image of disapproval.

"There you are, Mr. Galloway," she began. "And here we are, in an unacceptable state of disorder."

"So . . . what seems to be the problem?"

Chapter 6

"The problem is that your young . . . protégé . . . has absconded again. Leaving his class here on a Monday morning, unattended."

"You mean Shueyda?" he said, knowing quite well that she meant Shueyda. "I'm sure there is some explanation."

"Oh, indeed," she replied. "The explanation is that Mr. Momonen is unreliable and undisciplined. Setting a very poor example for these impressionable boys."

"But he may be ill, or in some other difficulty," said Galloway, for once in his life rather wishing an illness upon a person he cared about.

The headmaster, a diffident gentleman with a round head and very little hair, received a direct glance from Miss Booth that told him it was his turn to speak. "We have inquired at Mr. Momonen's lodging, Reverend Galloway," he said. "The other young men who reside at the boarding house tell us that he left yesterday, immediately after the service at the church, and has not yet returned. They don't know where he has gone."

"I'm sure he intended to return in time for class this morning, Mr. Jhowri. Perhaps he was detained, unexpectedly . . . again, illness or misfortune is a possible reason."

"If this had never happened before, Mr. Galloway, I might be inclined to believe that," Miss Booth said. "But as you know, there is a pattern of such behavior, which we have all witnessed. I realize that he is still very young, but this disregard for his standing obligations is simply irresponsible."

"We don't yet know that. I prefer to reserve judgment until all of the facts are in." He turned to Mr. Jhowri. "In the meantime, would it be helpful for me to take Mr. Momonen's class? What should the boys be doing this morning?"

"Thank you ever so much, sir, but I will take the class myself," replied Mr. Jhowri. "I am familiar with their schedule and expectations for today. And I will certainly inform you when we learn more about the causes of this . . . difficulty." The headmaster let himself into the classroom and the noise level dropped precipitously.

Galloway and Miss Booth moved away from the door and into an empty classroom across the hall. It was evident that she was not finished presenting her views to him.

"I realize that this young man is a favorite of yours—"

"Not a favorite, Miss Booth, nor a protégé. He is an able and dedicated worker and an apt student. Mr. Momonen is a candidate for the ministry and deserves appropriate respect."

"A candidate for the ministry? Mr. Galloway, you must be aware that the degree of maturity and authority required of a Christian clergyman is well beyond the scope of any Buraani individual at this time . . . perhaps some day, in the unforeseeable future. Another incident like this only demonstrates the unreadiness of the Buraani church for such a significant step."

"I don't agree, Miss Booth. Admittedly, we are hampered by the lack of a proper secondary school and college through which full seminary training might be provided. When we have achieved this, we shall be in a much better position to prepare young men with gifts and promise to accept such a responsibility."

"A distant prospect, of course."

"Regrettably, we have not the resources at this point to provide the formation and instruction that we might wish. But in spite of our limitations, God yet calls. And I have sufficient reason to believe that Shueyda Momonen is called of God and is being equipped to become a minister of Word and Sacrament."

Her face expressed nothing but skepticism, and David felt it was time to bring in biblical support. "Look to your calling, brethren . . . not many are wise men after the flesh, not mighty, not noble, yet called. For God hath chosen the foolish things of this world to confound the wise, and the weak things of this world to confound the mighty. Things which are despised, God hath chosen . . . that no flesh should vaunt itself in his presence."

"Well, certainly, and yet we do have standards for leadership in the church, which we neglect to our peril. Do you seriously suggest that a teacher who fails to carry out his duty to his pupils is in any respect ready for Christian ministry?"

"There is a degree of steadiness wanting, I acknowledge that."

"And the idea that we missionaries can devolve our role of guidance onto a Buraani church that is in its infancy is folly, of course."

"The American Mission in Egypt is ordaining young men as full members of Presbytery. And the Anglican Church of India has a number of indigenous priests now, and perhaps soon an Indian bishop."

Chapter 6

"Those countries have enjoyed the benefits of European and American influence much longer than this one."

"The Christian faith is no more English or American than it is Egyptian, or Indian, or Chinese, or Buraani. Western forms that have been introduced are mainly incidental and do not constitute the real essence of Christian life."

"Your enthusiasm for the potential of our Buraani Christians is commendable. But one also must be patient and prudent. Perhaps when you have served here for thirty years or longer, you will understand that." Again with her barbed reminder that she held seniority over him. He realized that her remarks about immaturity and unreadiness could have been intended not just for the Buraani church, but for him as well.

Shueyda did resurface later that week. At the boys' school, the long-suffering headmaster scarcely reproached him; Mr. Jhowri was only too happy to have his best teacher back in the classroom.

Galloway had opened the Thursday evening men's Bible study at the Presbyterian church in Adamu—normally led by Shueyda—when in walked the young man himself. The Bible study continued as if nothing were amiss. When it reached an end, David was annoyed to see Shueyda get up to leave. "Excuse me, Shueyda," he began. "I'm a bit surprised to see you here tonight."

"I usually teach this lesson," Shueyda said.

"Well yes, I know that, do I not? I came along to do it myself because you disappeared again this week and I could not know whether you would be here."

"Oh, Reverend Galloway, I apologize," said the young man, abashed. "You are quite right. I am very sorry for my oversight."

"It does make things difficult for others when you are absent, without a word to anyone. Mr. Jhowri has had to meet your classes this week. Others marked your absence and were . . . incommoded. It's not very considerate of you, at a minimum."

"I was not expecting it . . . just after the service on Sunday, I felt I should go to the village. The Lord prompted me. There was a need."

This was one of the aspects of Buraani spirituality with which David was not very comfortable. His ministry was largely occupied with administrative concerns, though he also took his pastoral responsibility for the care of souls very seriously. But there was a spontaneous mysticism in Buraani culture that arose like this, without warning, and seldom did anyone question the validity of an inner conviction of this kind.

"I do not wish to discourage your . . . awareness of the Lord's call upon your heart, Shueyda. It is important to be responsive to his will. But . . . perhaps you could have left word with one of your neighbors at the boarding house that you were leaving, and when you might be back."

"I did not know how long I would be away. But yes, I should have told someone. There was no one else about when I left."

"You can always leave a message with Julius, our porter at the Mission building, or here at the church. Verbally, or in writing."

"I am sorry to say that my attention was on the journey and I did not think of it. I realize that I made a mistake." Shueyda's remorse was real. "You must think me a perfect simpleton."

"No, not at all. I know you to be a dedicated and sincere believer, and a regenerate soul. All of us make mistakes at times. You must continue to be sensitive to the Lord's leading and attentive to his voice. You are like the young Samuel in the temple, and it would be very wrong of me to fall into the error that Eli nearly made. When you hear the voice of God, you must reply, 'Speak, Lord, for thy servant heareth.'"

"Yes, sir. I am sorry, Reverend Galloway. I shall try to do better."

But as it happened, Shueyda did not really do any better, not at this. He continued to leave abruptly on his evangelistic trips, often for days or even weeks at a time. Gradually, everyone else learned to work around it.

Miss Booth continued to view Shueyda's behavior as evidence of the basic unworthiness of Buraanis—even the truly gifted ones—for pastoral office. It did not occur to David that some of her resentment might arise from the fact that despite her many abilities and extensive experience, *she* was never considered a candidate for the ministry, purely on account of her gender. It may not even have occurred to Miss Booth.

So in that staggering week in March of 1910, when David was very close to the end of his rope, he also had a Shueyda situation to handle. Shueyda had arranged for Galloway to come to the village of Peshtaran on

Chapter 6

a pastoral itineration, even though, to the best of David's knowledge, there was no church in Peshtaran to visit.

David tried to postpone the trip due to the funerals for the McKinleys and Dr. Marshall, and the task he needed to complete for Mrs. Hardy, and the devastating abduction of the children of Kaskut. He was in no position to devote two days to this. But of course, when he attempted to contact Shueyda to reschedule it, he found that Shueyda had already left. What David got was a cryptic note from him saying, "Please be prepared to celebrate the Sacraments. Also, do not wear clothing of the color blue."

David knew very little about Peshtaran village. It was a tiny place, only about 600 souls, perhaps four hours away by horse or bicycle up the sluggish and shallow Meyhan River. A ferryboat passed that way every few days, but the ferryboat took much longer, since it stopped at every little town all along the riverbank, slowly loading agricultural goods to bring to market in Adamu. Peshtaran lay in the warmer lowlands of Yevladeh province that produced Buraan's cotton, sugar cane and wheat in midsummer, along with generous crops of tomatoes, squash, aliums and tender greens.

Peshtaran was a traditional Hanamid community by all accounts, conservative and cool toward outsiders. The American Mission had received no requests from Peshtaran to visit them, to open a school, or anything else, so it ranked low on the list of AMB priorities. However, it seemed that Shueyda Momonen had found a way to reach them.

Galloway packed his things and left Friday morning, inwardly grumbling.

As he rode on, however, he found it harder to maintain his querulous mood. The sun was brilliant, with just the right amount of warmth. He first noticed the sound of active birds, their insistent musical notes filling the air. Swallows flickered among the trees. Doves cooed from the rafters of houses where they were already nesting.

The young mare trotted willingly, also feeling the stir of new life. Along the bridle path, he began to see purple romulea and rosemary. Orchards of pale pink cherry blossoms and bright white flowering almonds appeared. In the wilder places, wisteria hanging from overgrown trees dangled like ornaments. And then in dooryards and gardens he saw the splendid Turkish tulips—fiery crimson, with long sharp tips of glowing gold.

Leaving the cultivated and settled areas, he moved through the wide meadows and open spaces of Yevladeh, and found them abundant with wildflowers, especially the stalky orange poppies, white anemones and masses of bold yellow broom. Against the frank blue sky, they filled his eyes with the vision of a beautiful spring that had somehow taken hold while he was crumbling under the burdens of a grim and painful time.

Before long he came across a small Hanamid shrine, whitewashed, conical in shape. Probably a tomb for the ashes of a local holy man or *pir*. Affixed on it was a polished brass sun with pointed rays, about the size of a tea tray. And below that, there hung a ceramic peacock, plumes outspread, mostly in a vibrant and glossy blue.

David reflected on what he knew of the obscure and secretive Hanamid faith. It was evidently an oral tradition, without books of scripture or doctrine, relying upon the repetition of a body of metaphysical chants known collectively as the *Qasidas*. There was a professional priesthood, chiefly responsible for the cremation of the dead. Often the Hanamids were described, perhaps unfairly, as fire-worshipers. But Galloway inferred that the sun as the symbol of ultimate divinity would easily lend itself to ritual involving fire.

The more disturbing element of Hanamid practice was the veneration of a kind of gnostic demiurge, whose symbol was the peacock. This being controlled the material world, in an antagonistic relationship to the divine sun: Tavus and Tavibus, the good and evil gods.

In addition to these, they revered seven lesser divinities, perhaps angels or spirits, each of them named in the cultic rites. And they also named seven human holy figures, saints perhaps, who had lived in centuries past and acquired a mythic status. It was hard to assess the Hanamid faith as anything but a polytheistic religion.

David was a good Reformed Protestant, from the long line of Scots Covenanters who settled in the Pennsylvania, Ohio and Virginia region, and anything that contradicted the Westminster Confession of 1646 would not go far with him. But he could acknowledge that his explicitly rational, ethical and doctrinal Presbyterianism was not gaining much traction among Buraan's Hanamid population.

Chapter 6

When it came to legalism, however, he was more at home. The desire to please God by eschewing sin made sense to him. He was aware that Hanamid custom was controlled by a number of powerful taboos, and he tried to respect them wherever he went. Among them, he knew, was avoiding the use of any shade of blue—a color reserved for the peacock god Tavibus only. Superstition or not, there was no reason to blunder about, giving offense.

Apparently, Shueyda Momonen had also come to this conclusion.

As Galloway neared the village, he noted its location in a green bowl-shaped valley surrounded by orchards and fields. The houses were all clustered together beside the river. He wondered where he would be likely to find Shueyda. Then he realized that the streets of the village seemed oddly empty, and he could hear voices a distance away.

He followed the sound of the voices until he came upon what must have been nearly the whole population of Peshtaran, gathered at a natural amphitheatre clothed with fresh grass. Standing before them was Shueyda, confidently preaching.

As Shueyda spoke, the people freely responded, voicing their participation. Galloway watched in awe. For a town with no church, they were putting on a very convincing display of corporate worship.

Suddenly, David understood Shueyda's frequent absences from Adamu, from his responsibilities at the Mission boy's school, and at the Presbyterian church there. For over a year—probably about eighteen months—Shueyda had been ministering here, at Peshtaran.

Eventually, someone noticed David sitting quietly on his horse above and behind them, and a swell of excitement passed through the crowd. Many people rose to their feet. Shueyda's eyes tracked them and he spotted Galloway as well.

"Brothers and sisters in Christ, let us welcome our pastor, the Reverend David Galloway. Please stand, everyone." With a clear voice, he led them in singing. "Praise God from whom all blessings flow . . . praise him all creatures here below . . . praise him above, ye heavenly host . . . praise Father, Son and Holy Ghost." David stared as the people vigorously sang the same Buraani-language doxology used at the Presbyterian church in Adamu.

A boy reached out to take David's horse. Others eagerly carried his baggage. He made his way forward to join Shueyda, who greeted him with deep bowing and folded hands. David moved in close to him.

"Shueyda, what has happened here?" he said in a low voice into his ear.

"We have founded a church, you see. Many believers are here now. The Lord has blessed us."

"But . . . how? I mean, not to diminish your abilities, but—"

"Oh, it was not I who did this, Reverend Galloway. Just wait a moment, you will understand."

Shueyda turned to the crowd of excited faces before him. "Sisters . . . will you come forward, please?" Four older ladies emerged from the gathering and stepped up shyly before the people. They were classic little Buraani grandmothers, very short and plump, wearing almost identical layers of colorful clothing and kerchiefs or veils upon their heads.

They bowed to greet David, their faces beaming with little smiles. "Reverend Galloway, these are the Bible Women of Peshtaran. Temla, Gansi, Neroah, and Famaar. These two are sisters, and Famaar is the wife of Neroah's brother, and Gansi is the mother of the husband of Temla's daughter." David did not really catch that, but it helped to explain how the four women looked so much alike. "Our Bible Women have been teaching the way of Jesus to this village, every day."

The transformation of Peshtaran was beginning to make sense. In Buraan, the village grandmas had access to every home and family. It was they who comforted the sick, who cared for laboring mothers, who brought babies into the world. They taught young wives how to rear their children, keep their homes clean, grow and shop for food, prepare meals, and look after their husbands. They attended to every domestic dispute, arranged every marriage, and stepped in to support the rejected, the needy and the bereaved.

It was only a lateral move for them also to become the spiritual engine of growth for village believers. But first, someone had to share the Christian faith with them, finding full acceptance and enthusiasm there. And then, someone had to teach them the stories of Jesus, ground them firmly in their knowledge of the Scriptures, and build up their life of discipleship and prayer. Shueyda, clearly, had done all that.

Chapter 6

In other locations, the ministry of Bible Women was becoming acknowledged and emphasized. There were many in Buraan, but seldom in Hanamid villages. Trained and effective Bible Women for this community represented a breakthrough, one that David in his limited faith had failed to anticipate.

"Sisters, would you please show us what the people have learned?" said Shueyda to them. After a bit of bashful jostling, the ladies stepped out to face the people. One of them began to sing in Buraani, "Our Father . . . You are in heaven . . . " And the people joined in, singing, "Holy is your Name." They continued, "May your kingdom come to us, and may your will be done here on earth, as it is done in heaven . . . Give us today the bread we need, and forgive us our sins, as we forgive others . . . "

David watched, and learned. Here was the genius of teaching a mainly illiterate people who possessed impressive powers of memorization. Simple songs, easy and uplifting, with direct and colloquial language.

As soon as they finished the Lord's Prayer, they began the Ten Commandments, again in simplified form. And then they sang, "We believe in one God, the Father of all power, Creator of the heaven and the earth . . . " And at this point, David felt his eyes fill with tears. If these dualistic Hanamids could affirm belief in one God, their Father, who created the spiritual *and* material realms, that represented a true departure from worship of the sun god Tavus and the earthly demiurge Tavibus. That brought them to the doorstep of a saving Christian faith.

"And in Jesus Christ, His only Son, our Lord . . . " They sang their way through the full Apostles' Creed. David dared to glance at Shueyda's face, and he saw there such a look of loving pride that his tears began to fall. It was like the look of a father watching his child take its first steps. Shueyda turned to him.

"In case you believe that all they can do is sing, let us test them. Beloved people," he called out, "What is the chief purpose of human life?"

Several of them chorused together, "Our chief purpose is to glorify God, and to enjoy him forever." The Westminster Catechism? Really?

"What standard has God given us to understand how we may glorify and enjoy him?"

"The Word of God, contained in the Holy Bible."

They carried on like this, clearly enjoying the overwhelmed surprise on David's face. When he shook his head in amazement, they laughed.

"Right, then," said Shueyda at last. "The sun has passed midday—we must hasten to the river. It will take time to do so many baptisms."

"Wait—baptisms?" David was taken aback. "Today? Right now?"

"Well of course. Many are ready. I closed the rolls at one hundred and forty. I asked the others to wait until the next time you come here."

"One hundred and forty baptisms? Shueyda, baptism is a solemn covenant, one that must be preceded by individual examination. It's not conducted in a mass event."

"I can confirm that these chosen are ready. They have confessed their individual faith."

"But how can I determine that, right at this moment?"

Shueyda stood silently for several minutes, watching the crowd, and then watching David's face. With great seriousness he asked, "Brother David, can you trust my judgment?"

At once, a nearly audible voice in David's head replied, *Yes*. Before he even had a chance to consider the question. Fortunately, David knew what that meant.

"I can, and I do," he said.

"Then let me advise you . . . the Spirit is moving *now*. Who can withhold water to baptize these who have received the good news with faith, just as we have?"

David looked out at the faces observing him expectantly, and suddenly he was among them, gazing up at him. It was more than empathy—it was a transposition. He felt what they felt, waiting for a decision on the validity of their belief.

"Brother Shueyda," he said, "It seems our best means to accomplish this is the river, though it will still be cold with spring melt."

"They go to the river every day to fetch water and to wash," Shueyda said, smiling. "They can endure it, if you can."

"May the Lord strengthen us all," David answered.

David went to his valise for his prayer book, placing his pocketwatch and papers inside the bag. He regretted having brought only one pair of shoes.

Chapter 6

He asked Shueyda to call forward those who were requesting baptism, and they arranged themselves at the front of the congregation. "Hear the words of our Lord and Saviour to his disciples: 'All power is given unto me in heaven and in earth. Go ye, therefore, and teach all nations, baptizing them in the name of the Father, and of the Son, and of the Holy Ghost, teaching them to observe all things whatsoever I have commanded you; and lo, I am with you always, even unto the end of the world.'

"Hence Peter the Apostle called upon the people, saying, 'Repent and be baptized, every one of you, in the Name of Jesus Christ for the remission of sins, and ye shall receive the gift of the Holy Ghost. For the promise is unto *you*, and to your children, and to all that are afar off, even as many as the Lord our God shall call.'"

The people murmured their assent to this statement, their faces expressing satisfaction.

"Doubt ye not, therefore, but earnestly believe, that he will number among his people these present persons, truly repenting and coming unto him by faith, and that this Baptism with water in his Name shall be unto them the sign and seal of the washing away of their sins, their engrafting into Christ, their regeneration by the Holy Spirit, and their engagement to be the Lord's."

The candidates for baptism led the procession towards the river. Green and flowering branches from the trees were passed from hand to hand, until boughs of color waved above every head. The whole village accompanied them to the water's edge, eager to witness this spectacle—surely the most interesting thing to happen in Peshtaran within living memory.

As they processed, they sang, "Glory hallelujah . . . glory hallelujah . . . glory hallelujah . . . in Jesus' name . . . "

David and Shueyda waded into the river, nearly waist deep. Shueyda held the prayer book and supplied the name of each person coming in to join them, often whole families with their children. Each candidate was asked to confess their faith and their desire for baptism, and then Galloway scooped up water in his cupped hands and poured it over the head of each of them, repeating the formula of baptism. "Meloud Enfer, I baptize thee in the name of the Father, and of the Son, and of the Holy Ghost. Amen."

He then placed his hands upon each head, saying, "We receive you, Meloud, into the congregation of Christ's flock, in the confidence that you shall never be ashamed to confess the faith of Christ crucified, and shall continue his faithful servant unto your life's end. Defend, O Lord, this thy child with thy heavenly grace, that he may continue thine forever, and daily increase in thy Holy Spirit more and more, until he comes unto thy everlasting kingdom. Amen."

It did indeed take all afternoon to go through this ritual so many times. The four dear Bible Women were the last to come into the water, standing together, and afterward embracing each other with tears of joy. The people on the riverbank waved their branches and cheered. It was a scene that David Galloway could never forget.

They finally hauled themselves out of the river and went to change clothes at the small house made available by the community to Shueyda whenever he was in Peshtaran. "Are you feeling all right, Reverend Galloway? That was a long time to stand in cold water."

"It felt cold only at the beginning, really. I soon got used to it. Are you all right?"

"Yes indeed, never better," said Shueyda. "As soon as you are dressed, we shall go and join the feast."

"There's a feast as well?"

"Oh certainly. This is like a hundred and forty weddings for them. Better than Shamsaal, the Hanamid New Year. The best ever."

"You know, Shueyda, the branches . . . that was very beautiful. We are only two days away from Palm Sunday. I feel that we have already been there. And all of this has taken place because *you* took up the call to come here and bring these people such joy."

"Well, you know, on that occasion, Jesus came into town riding upon an ass," Shueyda laughed. "It seems I am that ass."

The feast that evening was lavish and delightful. Evidently, the cooks of Peshtaran had been working for days to prepare their best dishes. Everyone in the village was invited, whether they had been baptized or not. David enjoyed it thoroughly, but soon retired to Shueyda's little house to get some rest. They would need to rise very early the next morning in order to visit every newly-defined Christian home before Galloway's return to Adamu.

Chapter 6

They did visit each family, so David could become acquainted with them, and so that he could satisfy his conscience that he had indeed examined each person for evidence of a sincere and saving faith. Perhaps it was the influence of their collective experience, but David had seldom encountered such emphatic and informed believers.

"So, Reverend Galloway, have you clarified your impression of Peshtaran's readiness to form a Christian church?"

"I have . . . there were only a few people who gave me pause. Meloud Enfer, primarily. He answered all of my questions with nothing but a grunt. I couldn't even really tell if it was a grunt of assent."

"Oh, Meloud. You need not worry about him. He has one problem—his wife Lilea came to Christ before he did, and he can't stand to admit that she could be right about anything." They both laughed. "I have persuaded Meloud to join the men's Bible study group, and from his participation there I feel sure that his faith is genuine."

"I'm glad to hear that. I have no further reservations based upon my brief interviews with the new members."

"Then you will be ready to celebrate the Lord's Supper with us before you go?"

"I think it would be most fitting. But I never thought to bring communion elements for so many people."

Shueyda smiled his gentle and somehow indulgent smile. "I took the liberty of making preparations beforehand. There will be bread and wine for all."

"Brother Shueyda," David began. "It seems impossible to deny that there is, in fact, already a church in this place. And *you* are their pastor, not I." Shueyda looked down, a bit embarrassed by David's statement. "I want you to know that I will recommend to Presbytery that you be licensed and ordained at once, and admitted as a full member of the clergy, with a call to the congregation at Peshtaran."

Shueyda's smile disappeared. It was a significant step, to become the first Buraani Christian to be admitted on an equal basis to the fellowship of clergy. He felt the honor keenly, and the goodwill of David Galloway in extending it. But there was a problem.

"I cannot easily express what this means to me, Reverend Galloway . . ."

"No, you were right when you called me Brother David. We are yokefellows in the Lord."

"But . . . I feel myself to be ill suited to the pastoral care of a settled congregation. I am an evangelist. That is my spiritual gift."

David considered this. He could plainly see the truth of Shueyda's words. "I don't deny this," he responded. "It does you credit to be aware of it. However . . . you should be able to conduct proper Christian worship, to celebrate the Sacraments, and to be fully authorized in the ministry of the Word. Perhaps you could think of yourself as an ordained pastor-evangelist. A missionary to your own people."

Shueyda Momonen looked into his eyes, and David realized that the two men were of exactly the same height. They were both too moved to speak. They embraced, and Shueyda wept.

They did celebrate the Sacrament of Holy Communion together, with all of the new members of the Peshtaran church, and Shueyda was right—there was wine for all, and dozens of little fresh loaves of soft bread. David made his farewells, but not before promising to come back the next week to observe Easter Sunday with them. He had no idea how he would accomplish it while also conducting the Easter services at the Adamu church. But he told himself that the Lord would provide a way.

The mare was brought to him, fed and saddled. He loaded up his things and departed.

The trip back through the blooming lowlands was a deep pleasure to him. The air was cooler today and there was a bit of a sharp wind, but he felt himself warmed through, glowing like a coal. When he thought there was no one else nearby, he raised his voice without restraint.

"Oh, when shall I see Jesus and reign with him above? When I hear the trumpet sound in that morning . . . And from the flowing fountain drink everlasting love, when I hear the trumpet sound in that morning." He sang even louder. "Oh *shout!* Oh, glory! I shall rise above the skies, when I hear the trumpet sound in that morning. Oh *shout!* Oh, glory! I shall rise above the skies, when I hear the trumpet sound in that morning . . ."

The sound of his rejoicing startled a flock of feeding sparrows, who launched themselves, fluttering madly, into the air.

2–9 S̲e̲p̲t̲e̲m̲b̲e̲r̲ 1925

Chapter 7

"Can you tell me, where is Mr. Flynn? He's needed urgently in the engine room."

"I'm sorry, I don't know, sir. I'll try to find him for you."

"Thank you, Mr. Agarin."

David Galloway had to restrain himself from moving much too fast through the buildings and the grounds. He tried to establish a normal walking pace, one that might convey confidence and the idea that everything was under control.

And in fact, some things did seem to be going well.

They had all come a long way from the "Cellar College" days. Some of their best graduates were now ready to serve their community as teachers. One of them was Mauris Agarin, instructor of music and director of the college choir. Galloway knew that he had been preparing diligently for the opening exercises. Thanks to Mauris, there was a fine new piano in the Assembly Hall. They were able to offer music instruction at every grade level, from First Preparatory through Senior Secondary. Young Agarin had a great deal of natural talent and was equally at home in the Western and Buraani musical traditions.

However, he knew nothing at all about diesel engines.

Two years ago, Galloway had hired an instructor to teach mathematics and applied physical sciences. Harris Flynn was quite a bit older than the other new instructors, nearly forty now. He was a veteran of the Great War who had served in the American Expeditionary Forces, working on the engines of passenger ships requisitioned into service to move American troops to Europe. He had not seen combat on the killing fields, but he spent some years at sea in all conditions, and troop transport was certainly not free of risk.

At one point, Flynn had considered a move to the ministry, and enrolled at Princeton Seminary. But somehow that direction was thwarted for him. He was reticent to talk about it—or any other personal topic, for that matter—so Galloway was not sure what went wrong there. Flynn grew up in South Carolina, and perhaps found the Yankee environment unappealing. But he had gone there specifically to study with J. Gresham Machen, another product of the South. David suspected that the problem was Flynn's prickly personality. Or his utter lack of preaching ability. Or his literal, humorless, rigid approach to everyone and everything. Not to put too fine a point on it, David regretted this hire. But he did need a person who could teach science subjects. And he also depended on Flynn's engineering knowledge to design, install and operate the new school's power systems.

As Galloway headed toward the administration and classroom building, he met Flynn on his way out.

"Oh good morning, Mr. Flynn. Sorry to interrupt you."

"Not at all, sir. Mauris told me you wanted to see me."

"Well, I was just having a look round the power annex, and I may be mistaken, but it seems to me that the engine is not ready."

"That is correct. The diesel fuel was to have been delivered on Monday. Here is it Wednesday and they haven't showed up yet."

"Well, of course, we will need to have the generator operating by this evening."

"And I know that, don't I? They swear to me on their honor that the fuel truck will be here this morning. I guess we'll find out what their honor is worth."

"Would you kindly notify me when you know more?"

"If you say so. It's too soon to panic," said Flynn, with an edge of scorn.

Galloway sought a reply to this affront but found no civil word in his mind, so he simply nodded and kept on walking. As usual, Harris Flynn either did not know or did not care how freely he offended people.

It was nearly nine o'clock in the morning, and already hot. September in Adamu meant summertime heat, which would not abate until October. But the academic tide must be taken at the flood, so classes would begin on

Chapter 7

the tenth of September, regardless. And the day before, September ninth, would be the gala opening and dedication of the wonderful new campus, with all of the festive trappings. They had exactly one week left to bring everything together.

Today would be dominated by the arrival of all of the boarding students and their families and the opening of the new dormitory. It was move-in day.

David Galloway paused for a moment just to look at the new buildings from the path to the power annex. Crafted of local limestone, they gleamed almost white in the strong morning sunlight. He thought about the long, long saga of acquiring the land, gaining permission to build, and conquering all of the technical obstacles to completing the buildings. The handsome central structure contained the offices and classrooms, with its tall windows framed by contrasting masonry and wooden shutters. The bell tower . . . the sound tile roof. The solid, spacious dormitory. The kitchen and refectory. The music wing and Assembly Hall.

He thought about the endless complexity of managing the laborers who dug the foundations, the skilled masons, the plumbers, the carpenters, the plasterers and painters. Knowledgeable stonecutters proved to be volatile and difficult people. The trade was dominated by two opposing ethnic factions: the Montenegrins and the Mitylene Greeks. Each sought to control the workplace, hiring all of their own kin. David's mild nature was not of much help to him in this instance. Eventually, though, he was able to direct them into a somewhat healthy competition, each group striving to build more quickly and more perfectly than the other. The fact that David maintained a fair distribution of labor between them, paid their wages promptly and honestly, and addressed them with dignity, led them to regard him with a certain loyalty and respect. Ultimately, they were easier to cope with than Harris Flynn.

Flynn made it possible to install a thirty-two horsepower steam boiler for heating the two primary buildings, with a system of steam piping to carry warmth to the rooms. He also set up the diesel engine and dynamo with wiring for electric lights—a radical departure for this provincial city, and one that David Galloway still could not bring himself to trust. The system also powered a pump and tank to supply the buildings with running water. The only building similarly equipped in Adamu was the American Mission hospital.

Was all of this new technology purely a luxury, a suspect self-indulgence? David himself had been content for many years with oil lighting and a little coal in the grate. But he had been influenced by the theory that the achievements of Western science served as a persuasive indicator of the value of Christian civilization. Calvin Mateer, mission educator in China, went so far as to argue that God Himself had inspired scientific advancement as a means to open the doors of heathenism, and gain the ears of the people to hear the Gospel. Mateer asserted, "Protestant missionaries are not only authorized to open schools for the teaching of science, but Providence calls them so to do."

Following this example, Galloway had designed a curriculum that required all students to apply themselves to algebra, geometry, trigonometry, and calculus. They studied geography, astronomy, surveying and navigation, with three full years of physics, learning about the states and properties of matter, motion and acceleration, current and magnetism, sound and optics. Surprisingly, most of the boys took to it easily, even though the more advanced classes were taught in English with American textbooks. Many of the students became adept at designing and building basic machines. One of the best science graduates, Mr. Barburi, now taught all of the mathematics and physical science classes that Mr. Flynn did not care to take.

Directing the teaching of chemistry and all of the biological sciences and medical subjects was the responsibility of the younger American Mission doctor, James Dillon. Now *that* was a successful hire.

As soon as David's thoughts turned to Dr. Dillon, he realized that in front of the dormitory building he could spot the man himself. He was one of the teaching staff who had volunteered to help on move-in day, organizing everyone, dealing with hovering family members, directing sixty boarders to their places in four bunkrooms. There seemed to be a disturbance at the moment, however . . . two boys were engaged in a clumsy and ineffectual fistfight in the dust. A crowd was gathering quickly.

Galloway drew close enough to hear what was being said, but stood around the corner of the building where he could not be seen. He knew that

Chapter 7

if he were present, everyone would defer to him, and he wanted to know how they would handle this incident by themselves.

Dr. Dillon's voice was loud and clear. "Boys! You will stop this right now. No fighting is ever permitted in our school."

"I will not share my room with a filthy Turk!" yelled one of the boys.

"Wait a moment, now. What happened in there?"

"I was moving in my things and I told him my name," the other boy said. "He pushed all my things onto the floor and started making insults at me!"

"And then you . . . ?"

"Well, I shoved him and said we should come outside and settle it."

"Apparently, both of you thought that was somehow a good idea. Did you believe that school rules end at the doorstep? Out here, you can just do whatever you like?"

At this point, shame was beginning to displace anger, and there was a long silence. Finally, "No, sir."

"So, what *is* your name, in fact?"

"Yusuf Kemal Behramoğlu, sir." Turkish to the core.

"And yours?"

"Costas Sinopoulos, sir." One hundred percent Greek. "Sir, the Turks burned Smyrna and drove out all the Greeks! Many people died!" The boy seemed to believe that Dr. Dillon was unaware of this fact.

"And you imagine that Yusuf did that?"

A pause. "No, sir."

"Indeed he did not. It's time that both of you learned that all of us at Hardy College are one community. And each of us is an individual, not a race, not a nationality. Do you understand that?" A score of baffled faces looked at him. James Dillon eyed each of them in turn. "I'll have you know that I have performed surgery and postmortem dissections on many human bodies, and never have I seen a person who was Greek or Turkish or Buraani or Armenian or American under the skin."

The crowd seemed to consider this.

"Yusuf, Costas, I want you to take hands right now." With palpable reluctance the two boys grasped hands, and Dr. Dillon placed his hands upon them. "You are bunkmates in Section Three, are you not?" They nodded. "I intend to assign you both to every work detail in Section Three, together, at the same time. You will learn to tolerate each other. If you are unwilling to do this, you shall go right now to find your families and head home with them. Take all of your things—you are not coming back. Your places will be filled by boys who are waiting to enroll. Is that quite clear?"

"Yes, sir," they said at once, in small voices.

"Very well, then. Kindly return to your bunkroom and look after yourselves."

The audience dispersed, and Dillon stood for a moment watching them. David Galloway moved from behind the corner of the building and stood beside him.

"Good morning, Reverend Galloway. Did you witness that international incident?"

David smiled. "How many fistfights so far today?"

"Just one that I have encountered . . . " Dillon slipped his gold watch out of his waistcoat pocket and glanced at it. "But it's only 9:45. Plenty of time for a few more before lunch."

"I like the way you handled that, Doctor Dillon."

"Oh, well, I was improvising. I am sorry I took the liberty of threatening them with expulsion. It's certainly not my place to make a decision like that."

"I doubt very much that we shall need to follow it with action. Assigning them to the same work details was an inspired idea. By the end of this week, they will be inseparable."

"I do hope so. But I apologize for speaking out of turn."

"You are the senior science master here. An attitude of authority is called for."

"Thank you, sir."

"Everyone is bound to be a bit emotional today, especially the new students. I would advise you to keep an eye on young Behramoğlu. He is one of three Turkish pupils in the student body, so the Greeks, the Armenians and the Buraanis may all try to display their incipient manhood by giving him grief." He took James by the elbow. "I want to thank you again for stepping up to help with move-in day. I do appreciate it."

Chapter 7

"Oh, certainly. And don't forget Mr. Agarin, Mr. Leyrenda and Monsieur Chevet. And of course, Mrs. Riley."

"Yes indeed. By the way, have you seen Mrs. Riley today?"

"She's probably on Section One, mothering the helpless little ones."

"Yes, probably! Thank you."

Ahhhh... Edith Riley! A great blessing from God. After the death of Dr. Felix Marshall, the American Mission in Buraan had struggled along for three years without a missionary physician. Then at last came Dr. Thomas Riley, an experienced general surgeon, and his wife Edith, a schoolteacher. They had met at Muskingum College in New Concord, Ohio. After that, Thomas Riley had trained at the School of Medicine at the University of Pittsburgh. It was Suzanna Hardy who discovered them working in the Pittsburgh area and recruited them for the mission field. Just another reason to be grateful to Suzanna.

Tom Riley was serious and shy, and did his best work in the operating room. But Edith's personality was just the opposite. Her oval face was plain and pale, like a boiled egg. But that face radiated kindness and care for everyone she met. People instinctively trusted her, including young boys away from home for the first time.

On each of the four bunkroom units there were fifteen beds for the boys and one for a resident assistant, a Middle Secondary boarding student who looked after them. The two-story building housed two units on each floor, with a broad stone staircase in the center, and doors front and back, for fire safety. Each boy had a wooden bunk with a fleece-filled mattress and cotton bedding, and a small nightstand to store his belongings. They were expected to bring their own warm blankets for winter. But it did not take long for the boys to discover that Mrs. Riley would never allow any of them to go without; a woolen blanket would appear on the bed of any child who needed one.

The new students on Section One were the youngest, and still bony, big-eyed and beardless. Mrs. Riley spent a great deal of her time with them at first. The Rileys were never blessed with children of their own, a serious oversight on the Lord's part. But Edith Riley leveraged this sorrow into the mothering of a generation of young Buraani boys. She was also a capable teacher, taking history and geography classes at every level. It was unusual for a female teacher to instruct secondary boys, but no one doubted Mrs. Riley's competence. She was also fluent in the colloquial and formal Buraani language, though with a certain Midwest accent that she was never able to shake, which the boys loved to imitate in an affectionate manner.

One of the youngest sought her out and waited until no other boys were nearby. "Please, Miss," he whispered. "I need the *pipu*."

She spoke in a low voice, too. "Each of the bunk sections has its own washroom, dear. It's right through that doorway."

The boy's eyes widened in disbelief. "There? Inside the house?"

"Yes . . . we don't use outdoor latrines here. There is plumbing in the buildings. Inside that room, you will find toilets, sinks and bathing plats. I'm afraid I can't go in there and show them to you. If you don't understand how to use them, just ask another boy in there. Your resident assistant is not here right now, but normally you can ask him for help."

He stared at her with a look bordering on horror. But she smiled at him warmly, and patted his shoulder. Gathering up his courage, he moved slowly toward the door.

Another boy was sitting on the edge of his bed, already quietly in tears. She worked her way gradually in that direction, taking care not to bustle over there and call attention to him.

She leaned down over him, speaking into his ear. "If you tell me what is wrong, I may be able to help." There was a long silence. "What is your name, dear?"

"Brovi . . ."

"Have you come a long way, Brovi? Where is your home?"

"In Osmaneyya, Miss."

"Ah . . . well . . . I know it's not easy to leave your home and go to a new place. I know that better than most, in fact. Is that what is bothering you?"

"No, Miss. I have . . . I have only my chemise and trousers here. I thought there would be clothing in my cupboard. But there isn't any."

"Oh, I see." This was not the first child to arrive with possessions so meager that he could not even produce a change of clothes. Often what they did own was dirty and in disrepair. Long ago, she had organized a closet of outgrown clothing from older boys, and such needs were always met. "Brovi, that's not going to be a problem. This afternoon, when we do

Chapter 7

the distribution of uniforms, come and find me. We have clothing available of other kinds as well. You are free to wear a chemise and trousers here in the dormitory, and of course a nightshirt for sleeping. Then when you are going to class, or to worship, or to meals and so on, you will wear your new uniform." She could see the tears dry in his eyes even as she spoke. "So you understand now, that's going to be all right. Just remember to come find me this afternoon at the big classroom where we will have the uniforms for you."

"Thank you, Miss. Thank you. Praise to Jesus."

"Yes, the Lord will provide. My name is Mrs. Riley. I'll be teaching your geography and history classes."

"Thank you, Mrs. Riley."

"I see that your resident assistant is back now. He can help you with this kind of thing, as well." Neither Mrs. Riley nor the resident assistant could correct the poverty of some of the boys' families, or the difficulties those boys would face in school comparing themselves to the ones with ample means. But they did what they could to help.

David Galloway was coming in through the dormitory entrance as she left. "Everything all right in there, Mrs. Riley?"

"Oh, the usual worries and predicaments, you know. This building is such a wonder, though, and no mistake! So thankful for this new campus! That place on Weyfour Street was a dirty, damp old rat-trap."

"That's putting it a bit harshly, isn't it?"

"Oh my, you know it's true. The Lord delivered us out of that affliction," she said with a twinkle.

"Thanks be to God," David said, also smiling. "Any special needs I should know about?"

"Nothing urgent that I'm aware of. I'm still learning all of the names, home towns and kinship connections . . . I'll get it all sorted in the next few days."

"Thank you again for your constant help and presence. You know how much we rely on you. It will be time to assemble for lunch soon, which will of course take much longer than it should, being the first go for the new kitchen staff. Then after that, while the school uniform distribution is going on, I will be in the office with open hours for all family members. If any of you need me."

A hot meal for sixty boarders and all of their accompanying family members was indeed a challenge for the kitchen, but it came off pretty well. The secret was to keep the huge vats of salted water boiling so they could make more pasta whenever they were in danger of running out. Greens sautéed in olive oil could also be quickly stretched, and when the fried fish was finished, that was that. At lunch, Galloway tried to spot Harris Flynn, but he was not there.

The numbers approximated a normal midday meal when the local boys, teachers and staff were all present. Sixty boys who resided in Adamu would join the activities tomorrow, bringing them to a total of 120 for the five levels of instruction: two preparatory and three secondary. Two further years of clinical education for the medical students took place at the American Mission hospital, mainly under the direction of Dr. Riley, and the head nurse, Fuleya Zaneen. And two years of theological training for the candidates for pastoral ministry were conducted by Reverend Galloway.

After lunch, the uniform distribution was prolonged and chaotic, but somehow everything worked out all right in the end. David Galloway met with one family after another, as he carefully worked to connect in his mind all of the new students with their homes and backgrounds. Returning boarders likewise often had changes in family circumstances that he needed to recognize. As usual, there were a few appeals for reduced tuition. Fortunately, Galloway could refer to a whole network of information sources to clarify whether the family was in a genuine state of need, or perhaps merely angling for a better bargain. Each of these students had to be referred from an American Mission primary school where they were known and their potential was assessed. Places at Hardy College were so greatly in demand that they had to establish an admission system based upon the student's prior work and likely promise.

As the afternoon wore on and there was no news from Mr. Flynn about the state of the engine and dynamo, David became increasingly concerned. At last, he summoned his office clerk, Mr. Tola, and asked him to find out as discreetly as possible what was going on down in the power annex.

Chapter 7

In the late afternoon, when the temperature had begun to moderate and shadows stretched across the grounds, they had outdoor games time for the students and their siblings. Mr. Leyrenda, the sports coach, brought out brand-new leather soccer balls and basketballs, badminton rackets and shuttlecocks, ropes for tug-of-war contests, and other equipment. Running around freely seemed to be exactly what all of the boys needed.

David Galloway kept an eye on the sports activities, but he was still preoccupied with the state of the diesel engine. Mr. Tola found him and explained that he had not spoken to Mr. Flynn, who apparently had dissolved into the air, but other witnesses reported that the fuel truck did make a delivery that afternoon. David sent Mr. Tola again to the power annex to make sure that the plan for the evening gathering was well understood. He said a silent prayer of thanksgiving and promised the Lord he would stop his anxious fretting.

He began to be more present in the moment, more attentive to those around him. Now when he looked at the boys playing, he felt acutely the joy of these young lives, their energy and freedom from inhibition. He had known many of the returning boarders, the older boys, for years now, helping to guide them through formative stages. It was a privilege to be a teacher. A privilege. Of course there were vexations, but there were deep satisfactions, too.

Dr. Dillon had returned to the American Mission hospital to relieve Dr. Riley, but Mrs. Riley was still on hand, working the crowd as only she could do. She patiently moved from family to family, learning everyone's name, listening to all of their concerns for their son in the coming year, reassuring the doubtful and making everyone feel welcome. David knew that he, as an authority figure, was less able to relate to the families on this level; his natural reserve and diffidence worked against him as well. There are different kinds of gifts, but the same Spirit, he told himself. Different kinds of service, but the same Lord. Different kinds of labor, but in all of them and in everyone the same God is at work.

As a deep summer twilight settled over the campus, the sports gear was collected and put away, and family units reassembled. Many of them had brought large picnic rugs to sit upon together, on the dusty ground. The College had some available for those who had not brought one. Eventually, everyone was seated on the ground, more or less prepared to listen to a few words. David opened with a reading from the prayer book, translating it into the Buraani language.

"Thou only wise God, our Saviour, with whom are all the treasures of heavenly understanding: illuminate all schools and colleges and universities with the light that cometh from above; that those who teach may be taught of thee, and those who learn may be led of thy Spirit; and grant that by the increase of knowledge thy truth may be confirmed, and thy glory manifested . . . through Jesus Christ, thy Living Word."

Many of the people replied, "Amen."

"New and returning students, esteemed mothers and fathers, dear families, and beloved staff, this is our moment of union and reunion. We are so fortunate to be here together to study and learn, to support and guide the young, to encourage and bless one another. And we are especially thankful that this year, gathering now in September 1925, we have this beautiful and well-equipped new campus as the setting for our endeavors. The generous giving of countless people has provided this facility for us. And in so doing, they have expressed their confidence that we shall all do our very best to benefit from it . . . to learn all that we can learn, and to give all that we can give. Imagine them here with us right now, on this lovely evening, enjoying it with us. My heart fills with gratitude."

David paused and looked at the faces turned up to him, barely visible now in the deepening dark. He nodded to a member of the groundskeeping staff who was waiting for his signal at the edge of the gathering. The young man ran off at top speed. "In a moment, we will share with you a special experience that we have prepared. It is of very great practical utility, of course. But I hope you will also see in it a symbol of the purpose for which Hardy College has been founded." There was a rustle of curiosity among the seated people. David now closed with prayer.

"O Father of Light, and Fount of all knowledge: bless, we beseech thee, this institution of learning, and grant that from us the light of truth may shine with increasing brightness on all humanity, so that wisdom and virtue might illumine our path . . . through Jesus Christ Our Lord, the Light of the World. Amen."

Chapter 7

David stood back and waited. A few suspenseful minutes went by. And then, suddenly, the buildings and grounds of the new campus were flooded with light. To say that people gasped is an enormous understatement. Most of them had never seen electric light before in their lives, and the effect was overwhelming. Massed windows glowing all at once, outdoor lamps along the pathways bursting into electric flame, strings of large glass bulbs festooning the trees instantly becoming visible as if by magic. Several people squealed with alarm and some young children began to cry. But overall, they reacted with a rush of awe and delight.

As the first thrill began to subside, the kitchen staff and other helpers brought forth big baskets of bread, platters of cheese, olives, sliced cucumbers, tomatoes, and peppers, and great bowls of fresh yogurt. The picnic supper was a tremendous success, and became an essential ritual in all future opening days of the new school year.

David found that all at once he was extremely hungry, and sat down to share supper with the nearest group, who welcomed him with giddy grins.

Chapter 8

Everyone was up early the next morning, especially the young boarders, who were still excited by the novelty of being together in the new dormitory. The atmosphere was like the first day of summer camp.

The primary objective for that Thursday was to move all of the classroom furniture, laboratory equipment and library books from the old rented buildings into the new ones. The students who lived in town would join the effort just after breakfast. Mr. Tola, David Galloway's office assistant, had spent much time arranging the hire of every available conveyance in or near Adamu to transport these things to the new campus. They were to assemble near the old rented buildings in Weyfour Street in mid-morning, just a twenty-minute walk from Hardy College.

Galloway kept reminding himself to expect plenty of confusion. He craved efficiency and considered his own time quite valuable, which he acknowledged showed a degree of vanity on his part. It was hard for him to accept other people flagrantly wasting what he believed to be of limited supply. He reflected on the fact that the Lord Jesus had only three years to save the entire world, yet found time to withdraw and pray, to dine with friends, and to observe the life of nature and the behavior of human beings. David was not sure how Jesus would go about moving a whole school-full of furniture.

The boarding boys swarmed the school grounds, yelling and running around, like boys. As the local students trickled in, reunited friends emitted bursts of joy and excitement, which they often expressed by wrestling and punching each other. Mr. Leyrenda, the sports master, kept the physical contact within bounds, and Mrs. Riley was again on hand to watch

Chapter 8

attentively for any boys who were being left out or finding it hard to mix with the crowd.

Galloway knew that this phase of community bonding was important, so he allowed it to go on for an ample period of time. Gradually they settled on the ground in the shade of the trees, and Mr. Agarin, the music instructor, got them started singing lively fellowship songs, such as *Heralds of Zion*. "Glad as the morning, swift as the light, heralds of Zion, go forth in might . . . earnest and eager, glad hearts of youth, soft hands of childhood, speed on the truth . . . "

David came forward then to explain how the day's work was supposed to go. The boys were organized into labor teams, each of them led by a designated captain. They would be responsible for specific classrooms and asked to carry tables and chairs, desks, lamps, maps, and crates of supplies to a certain wagon or donkey cart, bring the loaded cart to Hardy College, and reassemble the furniture in a new classroom. There would be prizes for the best work results. Chosen teams of older students were assigned to more complex tasks, such as moving and unpacking science lab and music gear, and reordering library books.

Energy was high, but it was sure to decline in the heat of the day. David hoped they could keep it going long enough to get the majority of the work done before everyone started to fade. "Let us pray," he said, and all of the boys scrambled up, joined hands and stood respectfully with their heads bowed. "Look upon us and hear us, O Lord our God, and assist those endeavors to please thee which today thou hast entrusted to us. As thou hast given us the first act of will, so give the completion of the work. Grant that we will be able to finish what thou hast called us to begin, to the glory of thy holy Name."

"Amen!" they all exclaimed.

A great deal of milling about ensued, during which the work groups were formed. The designated captains had lists of the boys they were to supervise. David noted with satisfaction that the two students involved in yesterday's fistfight, Yusuf and Costas, were in fact assigned to the same squad, and seemed to be behaving as if nothing had ever happened between them.

At this point, Mr. Tola found David in the crowd, and drew him apart a little. "Excuse me, sir," he began quietly. "There is someone here to see you. In your office."

"I'm very busy right now, Mr. Tola. Is it a parent? Can you ask them to make an appointment, please—perhaps for tomorrow?"

"Not a parent," he said, with a troubled expression on his face. "He has come from Aleppo and will be here today only. He says it is urgent."

David sighed, a bit annoyed. "All right, then. I'll be up there in a moment. Thank you." He explained to one of the instructors that he had something to attend to, and made his way toward his office.

When he got there, he found Mr. Tola already waiting. "He is inside now—I am sorry to allow him into the office in your absence. He insisted. And he will not give me his name or state his business."

Decidedly odd. "That's all right, Mr. Tola. Please go on back to the moving work. I'll join you as soon as I can." Galloway pushed open the door and went in.

He found a young man in his twenties, quite small of stature and very thin, with a mass of lengthy black hair. He was dressed all in black as well—trousers, jacket and shirt, like a Jesuit. Warm clothing for summer weather. Instead of settling on one of the comfortable chairs available, he was standing in the center of the room, hands thrust into his pockets.

"David Galloway? I have come a long way to see you. A very, very long way. Not just from Aleppo."

"You are welcome here, Mr. . . . . ? "

"I'm known as Gostan Hakopian. I work for the Near East Relief."

"Shall I ring for tea, or perhaps a cold drink?"

"No, thank you. But I would very much like to smoke. And I would rather talk outside, away from the buildings. Please. What I have to tell you is strictly private."

Galloway was more confused now. "Yes, all right," he said. "There is a shaded spot well beyond the power annex. I don't believe anyone could disturb us there."

"Yes. Yes. Please."

"If you'll follow me, then. This way."

Chapter 8

David led him through the rear door, out of sight of the work crews forming in the schoolyard. They went to the far edge of the property, down a slight incline along the wooded verge where a stream ran in the rainy months. The stone wall bordering the college was low and wide enough here to provide a place to sit, and it was somewhat cooler than the campus center.

Galloway sat down, praying silently in his mind. He truly had no idea what was coming. The young man immediately lit a cigarette, then paced restlessly for a while, apparently gathering his thoughts.

"I am not sure how to begin. Let me tell you what I am doing now: I am the director of placing-out services for the Armenian orphanages in Aleppo. I help the young people find jobs, a place to reside, and provide basic social and medical support for them as they reach the age of sixteen and may no longer stay in the orphanage. I have been working for the Near East Relief for ten years."

Galloway nodded slowly. Since the catastrophic deportations of 1915. Throughout the dreadful war years. During the chaotic collapse of the Ottoman Empire, the demise of the Sultan, the cruel ethnic cleansing of Anatolia by the Young Turks, the expulsion of Turkey's Christian populations into Greece, Syria and the Caucasus. This young man had been immersed in it all, as the Near East Relief organization attempted to mitigate human suffering on a massive scale.

"Actually things are relatively stable in Syria now, at last. Not like the nightmare years. We can feed and clothe and house and educate all of the remaining orphans now. Like me, they are growing up, becoming adults. Somehow we carry on."

The final desperate scramble of the Armenians from the Euphrates region of Turkey and eastern Buraan into Syria had taken place in 1922-23. So, two or three years of regrouping in Aleppo. Now this young man had come to Adamu to see him. But why?

"I think I can make you understand only if I tell you the whole story as I knew it. Please bear with me. It is not easy to talk about, and I don't really know you. But you have a right to hear this."

Gostan's body was tense, his face narrow and pale under the thick hair, which he allowed to fall forward around his eyes like a shield. "I was born in

Kaskut village. It was my home until 1910." Galloway began to catch on. "I knew the McKinley family very well. Mrs. McKinley was my schoolteacher. She taught me to speak English. I was at the church every day. Until that Sunday when the Turks came."

"Of course, I remember."

"Indeed. That day was the end of my world. I have been living like a wild creature ever since. I can't explain this, really." He shakily lit another cigarette. "I was inside the church when it began to burn . . . my parents rushed outside with me, and the soldiers shot them both. I fell to the ground and watched them die. Later, a soldier picked me up and put me on a horse, along with the other stolen children. There were twenty-one of us, all young but not too young, not babies. I was twelve years old at the time, but I was small for my age. They probably thought that I was only nine or ten. Among the children, as I'm sure you know, were Anne and Matthew McKinley."

"Yes," David said hoarsely. "We were unable to find them—to find you—or to learn what happened."

"That is why I am here. But you must wait until I tell it." He breathed deeply. "They rode with us all the way across the Anatolian plain, in the winter. It took many days. At various points they split up . . . some stopped in Konya, some headed east to Sivas and Trebizond I believe. They were looking for buyers for us in places where we would not be known. Anne, Matthew, Yulia Sarian and I ended up in a town near the capital. I will not tell you the name of it. There is a reason for this." Again a pause. "Yulia disappeared immediately . . . I could not find out what happened to her or where she went. Probably they moved her on to another city. But the three of us were sold close together, in the same neighborhood, even. Matthew was only five, so he could not do a lot of work, but he went to a baker who was tired of getting up very early every morning. It was Matthew's job to start the fire in the ovens while it was still dark so the baker could have coals ready for bread at dawn. In a way he was lucky, for a baker's boy always has something to eat.

"Anne was seven years old then. She went to the home of a well-to-do couple who wanted kitchen help. She started out scrubbing pots and pans, mopping the floor, you know. But this couple had no daughters, and they began to draw her into their family. After a while, she became like a

Chapter 8

daughter. She didn't work in the kitchen anymore, but lived with the lady as her helper, or dresser, or whatever ladies need. A closed Turkish *haraamlek*. It was hard to get information about her. Sometimes she veiled and went with the lady to shop or something, and once or twice I could have a word with her.

"As for me, I went to the workshop of a carpenter, where I started sweeping up sawdust, putting tools away, and sanding. Sanding, sanding, sanding for hours on end. I had no room, not even a bed. I slept on the dust in the workshop. If I ever seemed slow to complete a task, he slapped or beat me." Gostan's teeth were clenched. "One night he came to the shop . . . he smelled of *arak*, of alcohol . . . he took off my clothes, and he touched me. He made me touch him, too. I knew then that I had to leave. A carpenter's workshop is full of tools that one can use as a weapon, and I was sure if he tried to touch me again I would kill him."

David's mouth went dry. He watched the young man struggle to go on.

"So, I found a way to escape. I lived like an animal on the street, begging for a little food at shops, staying always out of sight. It was still so cold . . . there were other street children, and we used to form a group close together at night, like puppies, to be just a little more warm. This went on for a long time. Then, I learned that there was an American Mission orphanage not far away, in another town. Again, I will not say which one. I walked there . . . all day and night, without stopping, because if I stopped walking I would die. I had only a bit of life left when I got there. I just crumpled down on the doorstep at the back entrance of the orphanage, where they made deliveries. And while I was still alive they found me."

The young man shot a challenging look at Galloway. "And then I did something that might make you angry. I refused to tell them where I came from, or anything about me. Not even my name. Gostan Hakopian is the name I gave them, but it was not real. I also told them I was only ten years old, because I was afraid if they knew I was nearly thirteen they would not let me stay. I was small and nearly starved, so . . . I didn't speak at all if I could avoid it. I thought if they found out about Kaskut, they would make me go back there, and stay with some relatives I didn't even know. But my father and mother were dead and I didn't want to go to another home where I might be trapped, and treated as the carpenter treated me."

Galloway whispered, "No . . . no, I am not angry."

"But that meant I could not tell anyone about Anne and Michael. If I had told the orphanage all I knew, they might have been recovered somehow. It seemed to me that they were safe—better off than I was—and it was not clear to me then how much people like you would want to know where they were. I see now that it was wrong."

"You did what you felt you had to do, at the time."

Gostan shook his head. "May God forgive me. That is not the only thing I have done to survive. But I want to tell the truth now."

Galloway sat silently, letting the story unfold.

"So, living at the orphanage, those were good years. We kept it so clean, and there was a bed, and food. Also a nurse and help if you got sick. And I was able to go to the American Mission school, where I was so happy. I told no one that I could already speak English, because I thought they could use that to find out who I was. So I pretended to learn it for the first time, and I advanced so quickly that they thought I had a great gift for languages. Of course I also know Armenian and I speak Turkish when I must. It was a good place. This is a thing you know how to do well—make very good institutions. Schools, hospitals, shelters, churches, colleges.

"But this safe place was finished for me in 1915. The refugees, people running from the deportations. They flooded into the city. All normal work stopped and we did nothing but struggle to help all of the people.

"Much money to help them came from the American Ambassador, Henry Morgenthau, through his new Committee for Armenian and Syrian Relief. Mr. Morgenthau was a fine man, shocked and angry about the terrible decisions of Talaat Pasha and Enver Pasha. He went to see them so many times, asking them to stop the deportations, the killings. This was the beginning of the Near East Relief . . . they changed the name to include the Greeks and others who were also suffering. I lied about my age again and told them I was twenty—I was only seventeen—so I could do a man's work in the relief.

"They sent me to Konya to help Emma Cushman, the nurse at the American Mission hospital there, who was collecting orphans off the streets. She spoke Turkish but not Armenian, so I was able to help in some ways. You know, they told her to go back to America for her safety, and

Chapter 8

she said she would go if all of the children in her orphanage could go, too. Other ladies did this... Miss Graffam in Sivas, Miss Trostle and Miss Buckley in Marash, others. So many... I knew many of them. They were the only way that help could come to the people. Do you know Miss Cushman?"

"Yes," David replied. "Someone should write a history of the courageous women who stayed at their posts through it all to do whatever they could. Mabel Elliott, Maria Jacobsen, Nan Graybill, Edith Riley, Louisa Booth..."

"We struggled through the Great War and the terrible marches of people from the eastern towns and villages toward the south, driven into the Syrian desert to die there. At last in 1919 it was possible for the foreigners to travel again. That was when my languages were so important. My task was to interpret for the new NER workers who came quickly into Turkey from America. They had no chance to learn to speak new languages. So I helped them, from morning till night, every day, all the time.

"In Aleppo, I was assigned to Dr. Lambert and to Stanley Kerr. With Mr. Kerr I went out to the countryside in an army truck to fetch orphans who were being held in Syrian towns. Some were helped by Arab families... others were just used as servants and workers. We rescued more than 450 children this way. The Near East Relief needed to make records of all of them, so that the lost and displaced children could be found by their families. We made a big census of the thousands of children in Aleppo... the number was constantly changing, so I can't say exactly how many, but tens of thousands. Those who survived the desert marches.

"We made records for all of these children, with their name, the names of their parents, siblings and any known relatives, their home town, what they knew of their history as they fled. Stanley Kerr had the nice Graflex camera of the NER, and a stock of film, developing chemicals and photographic paper. He taught me to make photographs of each child to place in the record. This was the time when they discovered that I am very good at record-keeping. So I was no longer just a translator but a member of the records staff.

"You know that the British were in charge of Syria and eastern Turkey then, so it was thought that the displaced Armenians could safely go back to their towns. They were very eager to go home. So the NER started to plan repatriation journeys. We had some time to try to restore the children first . . . they were such a mess, so filthy, crawling with lice, so hungry and thin, clothed in rags that could not be washed, only burned . . . every one of them sick with eye and skin diseases, and their minds were stunned by all the death and suffering. Those who could not be placed with families stayed behind in Aleppo. But many adults and families got ready to go back to Anatolia. That was how I was sent to Marash."

"You were in Marash?"

"I was there twice, Mr. Galloway . . . and yes, through the siege. We did not know then that the British would give over Cilicia and the Euphrates to the French. So in the fall of 1919, I went with Mr. Kerr to Marash, to look after the five orphanages there. These were good places too, well organized, established by the American and the German missions. The NER took over the financing, supplies and administration for all of them, containing about 1400 boys and girls. Again, I was in charge of records and documents for all of these lost and orphaned children. I set up a darkroom and made photographs of them. We lodged in the home of Dr. and Mrs. Wilson, of the American Hospital. It seemed that we could manage everything there.

"But that was exactly when the British left, and the French did not have the forces or the will to maintain the peace. The Turkish Nationalists were furious about European occupation in Anatolia, so they began to organize and arm. You must know what happened in January of 1920—the uprising against the French. Suddenly there was shooting and shelling everywhere. Not just troops, but the Turkish population of Marash had been given weapons, and they moved all at once to attack both the French and us, the Armenians. They were determined to drive us out again, to kill and terrorize, to seize all of our property . . . to make their 'Turkey for the Turks,' just as they said." Pursuing their final solution to the Armenian problem. "The French were quickly overwhelmed and the killing and burning went out of control. People rushed to take shelter in the churches and in the Mission compounds, so then we had a new refugee crisis.

"I got separated from Mr. Kerr while trying to help feed people at the Second Protestant Church, on the western edge of the town. We were attacked in the street, and I ran into the old stone soap factory nearby. About eighty of us hid there and blocked the wooden door with a great round

Chapter 8

olive-pressing stone. The Turks burned the outer wooden buildings but two iron doors kept the fire from reaching the factory floor. We all kept very still and they thought we had perished in the fire, so they moved on to destroy other things.

"For three weeks, we were trapped in the factory. It was lucky that the soap was made from olive oil, so there were some vessels of oil there. We could consume this. Also, the company made *tarhana*, so there was some dry boiled wheat and dry fermented yogurt. Also a little *pekmez*, the syrup made from grapes. Not much, but enough for eighty people to survive on, just one mouthful at a time. But now, Mr. Galloway, I cannot abide even the smell of *tarhana*—it makes me retch."

The rapid flood of words paused for a moment, as Gostan struggled with his memories of the siege. His hair was damp with sweat, and his eyes were focused on the ground. He smoked constantly, nervously, and never sat down the entire time. David Galloway sat on the stone wall, unwilling to move or speak, so as not to interrupt the personal narrative being shared with him. He did wonder whether Gostan had ever told this full story to anyone before. He felt it to be a sacred encounter.

"It was so strange to have no idea what was happening outside our building . . . we could hear gunfire and shelling, explosions . . . and the whole town was full of smoke. We didn't know who was winning, who was losing, who was dying. Then, on the eighth of February, a young girl managed to reach us from the Second Church, with a message. She said that the French were preparing to withdraw—giving up the town to the Turks. Some French legionnaires were ashamed of this decision and secretly sent word to places where Armenians were thought to be hiding. They warned that if we wanted to evacuate we should go now. I brought out one of the groups from the soap factory, and we hurried silently in the dark as far as the Apostolic church. I left them there and made my way back to the house of Dr. Wilson. Later we heard that the Turks did overrun the factory and some of our number died there.

"Mr. Kerr was shocked to see me, as he thought I'd been killed weeks ago. The Americans were still mostly all right. Unsure what to do about the French retreat. Indeed, the French troops did leave on the night of February tenth, sneaking out like cowards, and about four thousand of the

Armenians followed them. It was a three-day march to Islahiyya, bitterly cold, storming, snowing. Even the soldiers suffered, especially the French Senegalese, who lost hands and feet to frostbite. A few of the Americans went with them to assist, including Dr. Mabel Elliott, but she could do nothing but watch the weak fall beside the road and perish. Only about 2400 of the people survived the journey.

"After the French departed, the Turks held a victory day, and finally most of the killing and burning stopped. We still had about ten thousand Armenians left to provide for somehow . . . remaining from about 25,000 who were in Marash when the uprising began. Most of the town was in ruins. Yet just at this point, Dr. Robert Lambert and Dr. Lorrin Shepard somehow arrived in Marash with money and supplies. They had become worried about the NER staff and all of the people and they managed to get to us from Aintab. They said that they had the protection of Kurdish militias who knew the Shepard family and had been treated at the American Mission hospital there, and that made them willing to help. Do you know the Shepards?"

"Yes, of course. Lorrin's father Fred was the surgeon at the hospital in Aintab and was a colleague of mine for more than fifteen years."

"Because of them, we could feed the people again. We began to set things to rights, as well as we could. Then when they left to return to Aleppo, Mr. Kerr and I went with them. That was in March. It seemed that the NER could maintain the orphanages in Marash again . . . but the Turks made it impossible. After one year, every Armenian had to leave Marash, and we moved all of the orphans to Aleppo. Mr. Kerr and I went back there to make travel documents for them and to bring out all of the office records.

"And now I work in Aleppo with them. There is a good program of training in the orphanages. They go to school, and many become teachers, government workers, office clerks. We teach them various trades—tanning and shoemaking, metal work, cooking and baking, raising animals and farming with irrigation, much more. Also carpentry," Gostan said with the ghost of a wry smile. "There is never enough clothing, so they process cotton and wool, weave cloth, learn tailoring and needlework, fine embroidery, knitting, lace making. I teach a photography class. With these skills

Chapter 8

we can place them into jobs and an independent life, when they grow up. Most of them do surprisingly well."

Galloway could see the young man relax a little, having completed this much of his story. But it did not seem to be the end. Gostan's mind was still working, still reading some information in the air, or in the dust around his feet. How long had they been down there on the edge of the campus? An hour? Two? David was not about to pull out his pocketwatch and look at it. His job was to remain still, and listen.

Gostan surprised him then, with a question. "What happened here, in Buraan, during the deportations? You still have Armenian churches and communities here. How can that be?"

"Some communities were destroyed, like Kaskut. Mostly along the northern and eastern borders, where Turkish and Kurdish irregulars were making raids into Buraani territory. The Nationalists may have had an ambition to enlarge their claim on Anatolia by laying hold of the entire Euphrates region, and they did gain control of everything to the east of Urfa. But we had two advantages here: King Shachandour has always been able to ingratiate himself with anyone, give a little, dodge a little, deceive a little, find a way to coexist. He didn't want to lose a vital portion of the most productive population in the country—most of the professional and mercantile class. And the other thing was the Vali here, representing the Turkish state. Ismail Bey is another skillful political operator and basically an honorable man. He saw the rampant destruction in Van, in Zeytun, Erzurum, Bitlis and the rest of eastern Anatolia. He didn't want to see it happen here. So between them, they managed to pour water on *this* house while the neighborhood burned."

Gostan fixed attentive eyes on Galloway for the first time. He clearly had not expected such a frank reply.

A rustle in the trees overhead. A slight cooling breeze lifted the midday heat. There was a scent of honeysuckle from the creek bed below, and the droning of bees. David was prepared to stay there as long as necessary to allow Gostan to finish what he had come there to say.

"Mr. Galloway, there is more. I did not want to tell you about this until I had a feeling, an impression, about you—if I could trust you. But I feel strongly that you should know this."

"You must do what you believe is right."

"Very well, then. I have been three years back in Aleppo now, and we have what is somehow a normal operation. Mr. Kerr has left—I believe he is in Beirut. Miss Cushman is in Greece helping the displaced people from Smyrna and the rest of the Aegean coast. Dr. Elliott is in the Caucasus with the huge NER orphanages there. Because of this, I thought that I could request some time away. I have been working without a break since I joined the Near East Relief ten years ago. They told me to take the whole summer and do whatever I wanted.

"So, I have been traveling to other relief centers, searching records of displaced persons and orphans, visiting schools and shelters. I wanted to see if I could find any of us—the children abducted from Kaskut. To learn what had become of us. I also went back to the town where we were taken, as little children, in 1910. The only ones I was able to find were Anne and Michael."

David's eyes widened. Gostan had found the McKinley children. "But how? After such a long time?"

"Well, it seems that very little has changed for them. I mean, they are still in the same place. However, they are not the same people. There is no more Michael McKinley. He is now a Muslim, a Turkish baker like his adoptive father. There was an elder boy in the family but he was killed in the war. So now he is the master of the bakery shop. When his father is finished, the shop will belong to him. He is twenty years old now, and he has no memory of Kaskut at all. He no longer speaks English or Armenian. He is a Turk."

David shook his head. He could not reply.

"It was harder to find Anne, because she is no longer at home. She grew up as a member of her Turkish family, and they arranged her marriage at age sixteen. Her husband owns a gentleman's clothing store—he is a skilled tailor and haberdasher in the European style. They are doing rather well. She says he is a good man and she loves him. They already have four children." Gostan coughed a few times, some dust in his throat. "She still feels a tie to her earlier life, and she thinks of herself as a Christian, but her children of course are Muslim. They legally belong to her husband. So there

Chapter 8

is no possibility of recapturing her former identity, and she has no desire to do so."

Gostan stopped moving about and looked David in the eyes. "That is why I will not tell you where they are, or their new names. They both made me swear that I would not, ever. I gave them my solemn promise. You must accept from me the assurance that they have made new lives for themselves, that they are settled and satisfied, and what's done is done. They are citizens of the new Turkish Republic. They are different persons. And I believe that there is nothing to be gained by disclosing this to anyone in the McKinley family. I do not believe that anyone else could locate them without the knowledge that I possess, and I will be burned alive before I will reveal it. This is what they want. If they should ever change their minds about it, they can go to the American Embassy and ask for assistance. The decision belongs to them."

David looked away from the young man's searching gaze. Tears were stinging his eyes. He had to acknowledge that what Gostan had said was valid. And it seemed plain that the information he had come to impart was at last complete.

"For reasons that we can perhaps never understand, God has led them to this point," David said. "I am deeply grateful to you for coming here to share this with me. I shall prayerfully consider what you have said. And my own heart tells me that you are right."

He slowly became aware of the hubbub of voices from the direction of the refectory. It must be nearly one o'clock, time for the midday meal. The morning work had gone ahead without him, one way or another.

"Please, may I offer you a meal? Some refreshment? You are most welcome to stay with us as long as you wish. I can offer you a guest room if that would be helpful."

"Thank you, but no. I can't explain my presence here to others. This report was for your ears alone, and now it is done. I would like to leave as soon as possible."

"Do you have a calling card, so that I may contact you in the future? An address in Aleppo?"

Gostan stood and thought about this. "As I said, what's done is done. All I ask... is that you pray for me. If I have wronged the McKinleys, I hope you can forgive me."

David swallowed hard. "As much as it is in my power to forgive. I will sincerely pray for you. And in my estimation, you have done no wrong."

"Thank you. Thank you, Mr. Galloway. If you will excuse me." Gostan Hakopian turned quickly on his heel and walked away, back toward the entrance gates. What's done is done. David watched his small dark figure move across the grounds. When he had gone, David remained on the stone wall, unable to go and join the active throng over lunch. After a time, he sank to his knees in the dust, resting his forehead upon the stone wall. A few leaves from the trees floated to the earth around him.

Chapter 9

Dr. James Dillon was not on campus that Thursday, when furniture was being moved. His dual responsibilities caring for patients at the American Mission hospital and also teaching biological science and medicine at Hardy College were sometimes in competition. He was a young man with plenty of physical energy, but he had not mastered the technique of being in two places at once.

The furniture-moving project was not fully completed on Thursday, for many inescapable reasons. So, the reorganizing of classrooms and offices overlapped into Friday. But for the most part, the work was done diligently and well. The teams that were most successful, according to the judgment of an appointed set of instructors and senior students, were rewarded with boxes of hard candies wrapped in brightly colored cellophane.

Friday was mainly intended as a sports and games day; thus, perfect timing was not essential. Hardy College had a strong commitment to organized games for the purposes of group cohesion, healthy exercise, and training in leadership and good sportsmanship. Returning students were eager to begin the new season with greatly improved facilities, and the new boys needed to start learning and practicing the skills required.

Also scheduled for Friday was the September meeting of the medical school planning committee for Hardy College, including both of the instructors in charge of medical training, Dr. Riley and Dr. Dillon. It was convened by the chairman of the local Board of Management, Manro Olorzey, who was really the reason why a medical school program had been established there. He had been adamant from the start that they would create a program that some day could hold its own against the Syrian Protestant

College, known since 1920 as the American University of Beirut. Olorzey, a wealthy landowner and highly-respected social leader in the Buraani upper class, continued to be the driving force behind it, making sure that enough resources were provided to make a credible start. His son Eyvor Olorzey was in the first class of Hardy College graduates to complete the practical training at the American Mission hospital and was now serving as a resident physician there.

Eyvor Olorzey and James Dillon were close colleagues and good friends. James was proud of the way Eyvor had performed as a student and a resident, and trusted his medical ability and dedication. If Hardy College could continue to produce more doctors like Eyvor, it would have fulfilled its objectives.

Thinking of Eyvor and his training drew James Dillon's mind back to his own years of preparation. Chemistry major and pre-med at Westminster, then medical school and residency at Johns Hopkins in Baltimore. Hopkins was in the process of inventing modern graduate medical education in the early years of the twentieth century: requiring rigorous study of basic science and extensive bedside training, imposing stringent antiseptic standards on the medical wards, admitting women on the same basis as men. It was a demanding place to train, but well worth it.

James was still a student during the Great War, and when he was finally ready to serve, the war was over. At Westminster College in New Wilmington, Pennsylvania, the very heart of missionary life in the United Presbyterian Church of North America, he had been confronted repeatedly with the idea of serving abroad. It required some serious soul-searching for him, but he felt he had something to give, and the American Mission in Buraan had the need.

He took passage in 1919. At almost the very moment he arrived, Dr. and Mrs. Riley left for their overdue furlough in America. They had been serving on the front lines of suffering throughout the years of war and deportation, keeping the hospital open despite famine, lack of supplies, crowds of refugees in dire extremity. Six years without respite. Thomas Riley had developed a chronic congestion of the lungs that needed attention. Both of them were utterly exhausted. The appointment of James Dillon finally made their furlough possible.

Chapter 9

However, there was little opportunity to gain any orientation to his new post. Tom Riley showed him around the hospital, introduced the staff, handed over the keys and departed. James was bewildered, suddenly immersed in an alien culture and language, and directly out of residency. He had never actually served as an attending physician before. Fortunately, the human body was basically the same here as everywhere else. He had brought a large shipment of up-to-date medical equipment and supplies. And the sincere welcome he received from David Galloway and the rest of the American Mission helped him to get on his feet.

It was only about ten days after his arrival when he received an urgent summons for a complicated birth. He fetched his carefully-packed obstetrics bag and set off. Much to his surprise, he was brought not to an ordinary house, but to the palace of the Turkish Governor of the region, Ismail Bey. It was a magnificent complex in a beautiful walled garden, like some Orientalist fantasy. Dillon had a vague notion that the Vali was the representative of the Ottoman Empire to the Kingdom of Buraan—more than an ambassador, the wielder of imperial authority. But he never expected to meet the man, much less to be invited into his home.

He was ushered through several huge, elaborately decorated spaces and inner courtyards to a sort of anteroom, crowded with people, all speaking at once in loud and unintelligible voices. He was presented to His Excellency, Ismail Bey, a dignified-looking gentleman in obvious distress. With the dubious aid of a number of volunteer interpreters, Dillon understood that his patient would be found in a private room through a gateway into a restricted area, separated from the public sphere by a huge and heavy curtain of carved chains made of wood, metal and semi-precious stone. The intense dispute before him concerned the conditions under which Dillon could legally be admitted to the apartment.

The doctor was not a member of the Bey's family, and was a male and a foreigner to boot. The Bey was consulting with advisors over the kind of verbal authority he needed to give in order for the doctor to be allowed inside. Dillon grew more and more anxious as precious minutes went by, possibly endangering his patient, who must be in a state perilous enough to justify sending for him and touching off this controversy in the first place. With difficulty, he managed to get the Bey's attention.

"Your Excellency . . . I believe we have two options here. You can allow me into the chamber, or we can transport the patient to the hospital. I would need to assess her stability before I could recommend transport."

"No, I'm sorry, no transport. No hospital. Out of the question."

"Then I urge you to let me examine her at once. Time is of the essence."

"One moment, please. We are near agreement. We have sent for the Ulema."

Dillon was not informed about who or what this could be, but soon, three or four elderly gentlemen arrived, and the discussion apparently began again. At last, the great curtain of chains was parted, and the Bey himself took Dillon through into the *haraamlek*. They passed quickly through several corridors and into a large bedchamber, crowded with women and girls, where another loud commotion was going on. They all bowed respectfully at the sight of the Bey, and Dillon seized the opportunity.

"Your Excellency, we must clear this room at once. I will need several supplies immediately, and probably more after a while. Is there a competent assistant here?" The Bey ordered everyone out except one short rotund lady, who was introduced as Fuleya Zaneen, the midwife. The midwife in turn had her own small assistant, who was tasked with relaying requests for articles needed. Dillon asked for a butane tank and a kettle to begin with. Ismail Bey excused himself to go back and sort out the discussion outside, and suddenly the big room was quiet and empty.

"Doctor," the midwife said in a soft and high-pitched voice that did not seem to match her substantial bulk. "Please. This way."

The patient was in bed, behind a large free-standing wooden screen. Dillon listened with his stethoscope to her heart and lungs, and did a quick visual assessment. She was not much more than a child, in a late stage of pregnancy, and clearly struggling. Agitated, confused, not making eye contact, not replying to questions, thrashing about and sweating. It did not look like normal labor. "Miss . . . help me, I'm sorry, I didn't catch your name."

"Miss Zaneen, Doctor."

"Yes, thank you, Miss Zaneen. What is the age of this patient?"

Chapter 9

"Sixteen years, Doctor. She is known in the palace as Küçük Hanem, the Little Lady. New wife of the Bey. In the eighth month with child. But the baby is already coming."

Dillon took the girl's blood pressure. Then, with alarm, he took it again.

"I need water for washing, please." She showed him a dresser with a pitcher of water and a basin. Taking off his jacket and rolling up his sleeves, he scrubbed his hands and forearms thoroughly, then swabbed them with isopropyl alcohol. The pelvic exam revealed a dilation of six centimeters. He raised the patient's foot and tried to flex it toward her; it sprang back forcefully, but the patient seemed entirely unaware. The ankles were swollen with excess fluid. "Miss Zaneen, is the patient urinating normally? Passing water?"

"No, Doctor. She passes no water in the chamber pot. See, very little."

From a leather pouch, Dillon brought forth a tiny pipe made of silver, wrapped in sterile gauze. A urinary catheter. With practiced technique he inserted it and drew out a small urine sample, into a glass flask. He measured two cubic centimeters of nitric acid into a test tube, then, holding the tube in a nearly horizontal position, he delicately poured a little urine down the side of the tube, taking care not to mix the two liquids. In a moment, between the two layers of liquid in the tube an opaque white zone appeared. A lighted oil lamp stood in a corner of the room, beside an armchair; he carefully heated the tube in the warmth rising from the lamp. The white zone remained. Albuminuria.

"Miss Zaneen," Dillon murmured quietly. "Our patient is critically ill. We need to allow labor to progress, so that after the birth I can treat her with medicine. I will prepare an intravenous solution, to use as soon as the baby is delivered. I would appreciate your help in caring for the infant at that point, if you please."

"Of course, Doctor," Fuleya said with confidence. "I know early babies. My mother was the best midwife in Afyon Province. I care for the baby while you care for the mother."

"Yes, thank you," he said, as they took up watchful positions at the bedside. "By the way, it's a great blessing to find that you speak English. I'm new here... I don't speak Buraani or Turkish, not yet."

"Yes," she said with a smile. "The American Mission School for Girls in Afyonneya. I studied English and I studied science. I want to become a proper nurse-midwife. But there is no school for nurses here."

"I hope we can rectify that very soon." The two of them attended to their patient in her sad and confused struggle, as Dillon regarded her blood pressure with increasing anxiety. At length, with a sudden rush, a very tiny baby was born. Fuleya received him expertly and moved away, while with a syringe Dillon administered an intravenous solution of magnesium sulfate to prevent seizure and bring down the dangerous blood pressure.

As soon as he could, Dillon examined the infant. The tiny thing weighed perhaps four pounds. His skin was thin, nearly transparent, and vividly red, coated with very fine, downy hair. No fat had filled out his bony face, and his ears were little soft flaps without stiff cartilage. His fingernails were barely developed. But he had a good strong heartbeat and respiration, the most important thing. Perhaps four to six weeks premature.

The period of danger for both patients was far from over. Seizure risk would continue for perhaps 72 hours, and the baby needed to strengthen enough to suckle reliably, once his mother was ready. He sent word to Ismail Bey of the successful birth of his son, requesting that the patients remain undisturbed for that 72-hour period.

James and Fuleya took turns napping a little in the armchair. He always packed a spare shirt and linen in the obstetrics bag for just such occasions, and a small travel shaving kit. He could heat water in the kettle over the butane flame, and shave himself in the enormous, ornately-framed mirror on the wall above the dresser. Fuleya slipped away at times to refresh herself—she was allowed to move freely about the *haraamlek*—and brought a supply of expressed milk from a supervised wet-nurse, feeding it to the baby with a dropper, mainly for hydration. The baby swallowed well, and they felt encouraged.

Late on the second day, the young mother rallied a bit, and was fully conscious at last. She received her tiny baby with joy. He suckled very weakly, however, and she became frightened and disappointed. Her blood pressure went up again to the point that Dillon had to administer another magnesium sulfate injection. Soon she stabilized again.

Chapter 9

Ismail Bey notified them that he could wait no longer and was coming there at once; Dillon knew better than to argue. He and Fuleya moved away beyond the wooden screen, and the husband and wife enjoyed a touching, deeply affectionate reunion. Dillon was a little surprised, as he had concluded from Küçük Hanem's age that she was mainly a plaything. He realized that this assumption was unfair. The Bey was delighted by a son as well, though shocked at the baby's feeble appearance.

"Doctor Dillon, my wife and son are alive, and I thank you very much for this. But he is unwell. So small and . . . and . . . " Ismail Bey probably wanted to add, "and ugly," but stopped himself.

"Your Excellency, I believe he is doing well, in view of his prematurity. He only needs a bit of time and feeding to fill out and gain strength."

"I want you to remain here until he becomes normal. He needs your medicine."

"Oh, well, actually, I was just thinking that, tomorrow morning, if all goes well tonight, I would hand over the watch to Miss Zaneen . . . she is quite a capable caregiver."

"No no no, the son of the Vali needs the doctor."

"Ahhhh . . . perhaps I'll just go back to the hospital for some fresh supplies, and then call each day to look in on them."

At this point the Vali's English failed him, and he had a hurried conversation with Fuleya. They gradually understood that Dillon could not in fact leave the room at all. The status of that chamber had been officially modified by the authorities as *salaamlek* territory, fully surrounded by *haraamlek*, like an island. Some hasty home remodeling had been required. Now, James was stuck in that room until the Vali decided he could leave.

As this knowledge sank in, Dillon's mind raced to adapt to the circumstances. He sat down to write a note to the hospital quartermaster, listing the items he needed delivered, both personal and professional. Then he wrote a note to David Galloway, explaining that he was unable to leave the Governor's house and asking that care be arranged for any patients received at the hospital in his absence. He gave these to the Vali and requested a cot to sleep on and another wooden screen for a minimum of privacy . . . and he reconciled himself to camping there until given permission to go.

Fuleya Zaneen was his staunch support during this peculiar captivity. She was also very good at training new mothers to breastfeed, and before long the baby had begun to nurse—not very well, but it was a start. "You are wonderful with both patients, Fuleya. May I call you that?"

"If you wish, Doctor Dillon."

"Please call me James. After all, we are practically living together."

"Yes, Doctor James." He realized that, culturally, he was out of his depth.

Fuleya tried to help him, starting his language learning right there in the sickroom. She slowly taught him terms for the parts of the body, in Turkish and Buraani. She taught him words that denote common maladies: headache, cough, nausea, fever, itching, diarrhea, various kinds of pain. Problems that patients were likely to present. She taught him basic conversational phrases and polite conventions of speech.

In return, he began to teach her standard nursing skills, medical nomenclature, the basic assumptions and practices of inpatient management. His determination to initiate a respectable nursing program at Hardy College was firmly reinforced by this experience.

After two and a half long weeks, Ismail Bey conceded that perhaps his dear wife and little Iskender, their son, would survive without him, so Dr. Dillon was permitted to leave. Iskender was feeding well, putting on a little weight, opening his eyes at times; his skin and muscle tone had greatly improved. He now looked like, if not a full-term baby, at least a baby, and not some red wrinkled gnome.

When Ismail Bey came to escort Dillon out of the palace, he brought a book-sized box covered in plush black velvet, and presented it to him. Inside was a lovely gold pocketwatch, with a baroque gold chain. Words were engraved on the back in fine Ottoman Turkish calligraphy. It said "Dillon Hekim" . . . Dillon the wise, the learned physician. James was a bit embarrassed and showed it to David Galloway as soon as he returned, offering to sell it and donate the proceeds to the hospital. David pointed out that it would be impolitic to reject a gift from the Vali, and that the item had a personal inscription. Prudent to keep it and to bring it out to be seen whenever the Vali was near.

Chapter 9

David was right about the importance of the Governor's favor. Ismail Bey never forgot Dillon's help. He used his influence on behalf of the American Mission from that point forward, subtly enabling the purchase of land and building permits for the new College, manipulating the bureaucracy on behalf of the Mission schools and hospital. James served as little Iskender's pediatrician.

And now, six years later, they were ready to celebrate the gala opening of Hardy College. A special dinner party was planned for Saturday evening, for the members of the American Mission in Buraan. They were gathering from all points of the country for this event.

David Galloway still resided in two small rooms above the Mission offices, so the Rileys volunteered to host the dinner at their large house beside the hospital. They planned a holiday dinner buffet of American-style dishes, a nostalgic treat, especially for those who lived in outlying villages where such meals were seldom seen. Roast turkey, ham, prime rib of beef, scalloped potatoes, Harvard beets, bowls of fresh peas, yeast rolls and corn bread with butter, even apple pie, using apples imported from Europe. Everyone dressed in their best and came to the party in a festive mood.

David noticed that during the dinner, James Dillon seemed a bit distracted. He kept pulling out that gold pocketwatch to check the time. After dessert was served and people were moving about having tea and coffee, precisely at 8:30 pm, someone arrived at the front door. James moved quickly to the foyer. When he returned, he was bringing another guest: the daughter of Manro Olorzey, sister to his colleague Eyvor.

Many of those present knew her, as Manro was such a prominent member of the Christian community there, and Marya herself worked for the Mission, teaching at the American School for Girls in Adamu. Some had known her since she was a little girl. She had grown into a beautiful young woman, slender, dark, graceful, with a gentle and charming personality. She was elegantly dressed. A few faces betrayed discomfort, however, as this dinner was meant just for the Americans, and she had evidently not been invited.

While all faces were turned toward them, James cleared his throat a bit. "Friends, brothers and sisters of the Mission, whilst we are all gathered together, this seems like the perfect time to share with you some very exciting news. Allow me to present to you my fiancée, Marya Olorzey."

The silence that followed this announcement was profound.

A few very awkward seconds went by. The first to step forward, with a warm smile, was Edith Riley. "How wonderful, my dears! How wonderful! So very happy for you! Welcome to the family, Marya."

Then from a corner of the room, an angry voice exploded. "What on earth? What can you possibly be thinking?" All heads swiveled in that direction. Harris Flynn, the College engineer and physical sciences master, was swelling up like a bullfrog. His hands were clenched into actual fists. "This is an outrage! What is the matter with you people?"

The room reacted as people do at the first perception of an earth tremor. Their faces went blank, and they looked around at each other, not quite believing what their senses told them. "This is modernism! Liberalism! Not the faith of our fathers. You people don't seem to know the difference anymore." Flynn's voice was harsh.

"It's unthinkable that we should accept such intimacy with the colored races. We must endure table fellowship, and sometimes even lodging in the same locations, sharing lavatories and the like. But this kind of thing is an affront to God and the intention of the Creator. We were made as separate races and only the godless liberals can imagine that such a thing can be tolerated!"

Flynn forged ahead. "While I was at Princeton, I learned what happened when they planned to integrate the dormitory with a colored student. Professor Machen objected in the strongest terms. He would move out himself rather than permit such equality and intimacy. Professor Warfield was going on glibly about the civil rights of Negroes, as if that were in any way the salient point, or a valid consideration. There are other seminaries that such a student can attend, among his own kind. The mixing of races is folly, and certainly marriage is beyond any limits. Surely even the desire to marry such a woman is basically depraved."

James Dillon was coming back to life. "Now just a minute, Mr. Flynn—"

"It's time you learned to appreciate the facts of human nature, Dr. Dillon. You're a disgrace to the American Mission! What would we be teaching

Chapter 9

these people here, if we abandon the God-given superior status of the white man in such a shameless fashion? This is subversion, a threat to our prestige, a public sign of degeneration and moral decay. Perhaps you don't know any better. But this behavior discredits all of us. It's not just your personal pleasures at stake."

Poor Marya looked as if she had been slapped, or perhaps electrocuted. She first shrank closer to James, clutching his hand, then unconsciously began stepping backward, retreating toward the door.

"And I suppose you haven't given a thought to the wretched offense of producing children of mixed racial descent. That degrades not only you, but the entire population. You have a basic responsibility to preserve and promote our Western way of life. I can't imagine what you think you are doing here in this country, if not that!"

David Galloway was slow to respond to this scene, overcome by a feeling of shock. "Mr. Flynn, I insist that you control yourself at once."

"Reverend Galloway, I consider that you also are to blame for this failure of standards and discipline. You have fostered the kind of liberalism here that substitutes secular ethical principles for the eternal Word of God. The line of cleavage between liberalism and Christianity is ever and often transgressed in our organization. It's your Social Gospel, your aim to transform the organism of cultural life instead of rescuing these benighted souls ... *that* has brought us to this pretty pass, sir! You believe that applied religion is all there is of Christianity, that it is merely a model of behavior. That God exists for the benefit of man, that human institutions, the society and the state, can be perfected into the peaceable kingdom."

Flynn was shaking his fists now, a parody of righteous indignation. "Why, you're even friendly with the Catholics and the Orthodox here, right here under our noses! They're no better than heathen! Wickedness and folly, sir, and a betrayal of your sacred call!"

"Mr. Flynn. Please leave this house *now*. We shall meet on Monday in my office and determine whether you have any further place in the American Mission." Galloway spoke coldly. "If you are not prepared then to repent sincerely and make amends, I shall require your resignation."

"As if *you* have the capacity to judge *me*. You, sir—and the rest of you—" Flynn sputtered, gesturing toward the others in the room.

"That is quite enough," said Galloway, moving toward him.

"Don't you dare come near me. I am leaving." With a glare at James and Marya, Flynn stalked toward the door. Everyone pulled away from him as he passed.

The door slammed. There was an audible exhalation, for many had been holding their breath. Galloway needed to address them immediately. "I am so very sorry that all of you had to witness that. Our colleague is . . . *non compos mentis*. And I apologize most of all to you, James and Marya. You are beloved members of this community and it grieves me bitterly that you were abused in such a manner." Galloway's voice broke. "I wish to say . . . your happy news . . . "

Edith Riley extended her hands to the couple. "I am sure that I speak for all of us when I say that we are delighted by your engagement, and I for one wish to hear every detail. Please come sit by me at the table and tell me all about it. Everyone, there is more apple pie to come, and some other nice desserts, and we shall make fresh coffee and tea. Come along now, friends."

The party regained some of its momentum. In low voices, people processed together what they had seen and heard. The incident seemed to have the perverse effect of uniting the group around Dr. Dillon and Miss Olorzey, in a way that might have been unlikely before.

This was the first such relationship in the American Mission ranks, and some other staff members were uncomfortable with it. In the past, a young man would seldom be sent into the mission field without an American wife, to establish an exemplary Christian household, to serve as an unpaid and unofficial worker, and to prevent the husband from straying after temptation. These were believed to be important functions. Ever since the earliest days of exploration and empire, men had availed themselves of local companionship, so to speak. It was a perennial problem. People held numerous, often unspoken, opinions about it.

When the time came for the guests to leave, James and Marya were pressed into a sort of receiving line, as each person or couple passed by and offered their affection and best wishes. Finally, Tom and Edith Riley, David Galloway, James and Marya were the only ones left. They all held hands and prayed together, not *pro forma* but in an expressive, emotional, and deeply personal way.

Chapter 9

James thanked each of them for their support. Then he said, "Sometimes I do wonder what I am doing here in Buraan. I could be setting bones and delivering babies in Youngstown, Ohio. But I feel deep in my soul that it is a blessed thing to help those in need, the sick and the injured, and for some reason God has given me the people here in Buraan to work for. If the folks back home in Youngstown could know the intense satisfaction that it gives me to relieve pain and assist those suffering and dying, in *this* place, where the people owe me nothing . . . I don't know, it feels so *holy*. And now I have found even greater happiness here."

Marya spoke up then. "I thank you as well. And we both apologize for failing to let you know that I was coming tonight. It was meant to be a pleasant surprise. We thought that if I joined you after dinner you would not need to prepare for another guest, Mrs. Riley. We didn't anticipate . . . the result."

"Never you mind, my dear. I'm so glad you came. James, see this young lady safely home. And we shall meet again in church tomorrow." She smiled and embraced the two young people, but her empathetic heart was aching for them. After all of the guests had gone, Tom Riley put his arms around his wife, and held her close while she quietly wept.

Chapter 10

David Galloway spent a sleepless night reliving that incident at the Rileys' house. He kept scolding himself for being too slow to rise to Dillon's defense, for being clumsy and inarticulate, for hiring Flynn in the first place, and for keeping him on the staff even after it became clear that he was an unhappy man who managed to spread unhappiness everywhere he went.

David lay there in the dark, sifting through each incident with Flynn over the past two years, searching for a way he could have handled it better, perhaps helped Flynn to adapt, or mature, or whatever it was he needed. He had not loved Flynn enough. Enough to help him become, as St Paul said, "transformed by the renewing of your mind." However, David knew that it was always easy for him to see how someone else needed to repent and be changed, while at the same time the other person was doubtless thinking the same way about him.

Had Galloway overlooked Flynn's maladjustment in order to get what he wanted—the power systems for the new school compound? Perhaps he had used the poor man for his own vainglorious ends.

Eventually he got out of bed, knelt and prayed humbly for help. David was normally very critical of himself and his own shortcomings. He seemed to find a great deal to pray about.

But Sunday morning arrived right on schedule, whether Galloway had slept well or not.

The service for the Lord's Day at Adamu Presbyterian Church was going to demand his full attention. There would be the usual ample crowd, plus all of the American Mission colleagues who had come from their own

Chapter 10

stations for last night's festive dinner and the other events surrounding the dedication of the new campus of Hardy College, plus others coming into town for this occasion. His sermon was ready and the liturgy planned, but he felt some pressure to make this service a special one.

Leaving the Mission office building with its thick stone arches and high ceilings, Galloway was struck by a wall of heat, and the palpable weight of the sun. Another day of summer weather. He was wearing a lightweight woolen suit, dark and sober enough for Sunday, with black leather oxfords, shirt collar high and very tight, a dark narrow tie. Not well designed for a Buraani heatwave. By the time he completed the ten-minute walk to the church, his skin was slick and prickling with heat.

He could take off his jacket in the vesting room and immediately did so. Hearing someone enter the room behind him, he assumed it was the attendant bringing him a cool drink. "Thank you, Rosha," he said, turning around. Though it was not Rosha the tea boy, but Shueyda Momonen, the assistant pastor of the Adamu church.

"Oh, good morning, Brother Shueyda," he said quickly. "How are you? Everything all right?"

"Yes indeed, Brother David, the Lord be praised," said Shueyda. "I am well and prepared for worship. But—if I may say so—you seem a bit out of sorts."

"The heat," said David. "I am ready for it to be over now. It takes the starch out of me."

"A few weeks longer. The Lord chastens those whom he loves."

"Well . . . yes, I suppose so. Now this morning, you will lead the hymns in English and Buraani, is that right? And read the Scriptures?"

"I shall lead the hymns, but we have asked Brother Whittaker, who is here visiting from Osmaneyya, to read the lessons."

"Good idea. And about the services for Wednesday . . . "

"We need to discuss this. A difficulty has arisen."

Oh no, what now? "Umm . . . I don't think there is time to get into anything at the moment, Brother Shueyda . . . can you stay for a while after the service? Meet me in the office?"

"Yes, of course. It should not take long."

"Thank you. I believe it's time for the congregational singing to begin."

Shueyda went off to the sanctuary, where scores of people were already assembled, to lead about forty minutes of chanting and singing before the formal service began. Buranni congregations lived for the music. Through it they expressed their deepest emotional and spiritual feelings, and received a primal experience of pleasure. There was a great deal of musical talent in the community. They skillfully modified Western hymns and gospel songs both in English and in translation, along with Buraani traditional folk forms. They employed the ancient Hanamid chanting of *Qasidas* and other sacred texts, adapted to convey Bible stories and themes. Shueyda expertly led them through one song after another, as more and more congregants arrived and squeezed into the already crowded pews.

David went over the plan for the service carefully, and reviewed the sermon in his mind. He tried hard to tune out all of the anxieties and concerns around him and focus fully on the Gospel message . . . with limited success.

At the appointed hour, Galloway put on his heavy, deeply-pleated, black Geneva pulpit robe, with broad bands of thick black velvet down the front. It was like wearing a quilt or blanket over his clothing. He entered from the sacristy, and the moment he opened the door, a flood of superheated moist air enveloped him. The pews were packed with warm bodies, and most of them had been sitting there for an hour already, radiating heat, singing with their warm breath. Many of the people had small paper fans in their hands and were trying to stir the steamy air around them.

Shueyda gestured for the people to stand, and they sang, "Praise God from whom all blessings flow . . ."

Some of the older people were not able to stand and remained seated, and among them David spotted Louisa Booth. His venerable colleague, now seventy-five years old, suffered from arthritis in her hips and rarely left her lodging anymore. But she was there for this occasion. He immediately regretted the weakness that had tempted him to be cross about a couple of hours spent in an overheated room, considering what Louisa had been through.

Miss Booth had come to Buraan late in the previous century as a missionary schoolteacher. She accepted greater and greater responsibility until she was accountable for oversight of all of the primary schools, both day

Chapter 10

and boarding, of the American Mission in Buraan. It was a demanding administrative task, as great as that of any of the men who had served there. She had remained at her post throughout the Great War, even though the Mission and local officials urged American school staff to leave for their own safety. She refused to budge unless all of the children in her schools could be guaranteed their safety as well.

When instruction became impossible and deportations tore up the social fabric of the region, she turned school buildings into hospitals and shelters for orphans. She and many other teachers joined the nurses in caring for the wounded, the sick, the emaciated and destitute people of all nationalities. Hunger and the constant threat of violence gripped them all; she barely survived a bout of typhus that killed countless pupils, colleagues and friends.

An imposing woman who spoke all of the local languages capably, she took upon herself the particular cause of insisting that officials of every government provide the supplies she needed to feed her many dependents, protect the Mission premises from attack, and subvert the deportation regime in every way possible. They all learned to spare themselves vexation by submitting to her.

After the War, her mind began to unravel . . . slowly at first, and then with a swift plunge into dementia. That and the burden of constant pain kept her chiefly housebound. She had a full-time squad of Buraani and Armenian helpers who cared for her needs, kept her company, and endured her often very irascible moods. She spoke only a little now, but still barked at her helpers and expected their instant compliance.

David was a bit surprised to see her at the church that morning, knowing what an ordeal it was for her to get from place to place, forcing her legs to move with the help of two crutches, refusing to accept a wheeled chair or any but the most inescapable assistance. Someone must have thought it was fitting for her to be there. And despite her disagreeable behavior, she was treated by everyone with the utmost respect.

He began the invocation. "Eternal God, our Maker and our Lord, Giver of all grace, from whom every good thing cometh, and who pourest thy Spirit upon all who seek thee: deliver us, when we draw nigh to thee, from coldness of heart and wanderings of mind; that with steadfast thoughts and pure affections we may worship thee in spirit and in truth. Through Jesus Christ our Lord. Amen."

More singing, many prayers, psalms, confession of sin, assurance of pardon, recitation of the creed. Adoration, thanksgiving, supplication, intercession. More hymns. Presbyterians stood second to none in the crafting of meticulous liturgies for worship, with a concomitant emphasis on reading, hearing and teaching from the Word. At the lectern, Rev. Whittaker read the Scripture passages, first Psalm 145, then the fourth chapter of Second Kings, culminating in the story of the Feeding of the Five Thousand from the Gospel of Matthew, chapter fourteen.

By the time Galloway entered the pulpit to preach, everyone in the room was drenched in sweat. Traditional worship under these conditions was like an endurance event. As he stood in the pulpit leading the dedicatory prayer, as luck or providence would have it, a beam of sunlight from a very high window slanted down directly upon his head.

David Galloway was now a distinguished-looking gentleman of fifty-three, the classic image of a cultured member of the clergy. His hair was graying first at the crown instead of at the temples, as with many men of his age; when the streak of sun hit him it made the top of his head light up like a halo. For many in the congregation, this seemed an auspicious and gratifying sign.

"Dearest brethren, how joyful we are to welcome today not only the members of our beloved congregation, but so many guests and visitors from out of town. It is a great blessing to have you worshiping among us this morning." David scanned the sea of faces turned up towards him, making eye contact with as many as he could. As he did so, he noticed something odd: Louisa Booth was scowling fiercely and twisting in her seat. Her attendants were trying to restrain her, which made her more agitated. She yanked her hands away from them as they tried gently and repeatedly to hold her hands or wrists.

"I can't help but compare this abundance before us, so many faithful believers coming together to worship Christ, with the modest beginnings of our ministry here . . . the few people who heard the call and came to this neglected land, bringing good news of salvation and eternal life. We know who those bold pioneers were, and we honor their memory, especially those

Chapter 10

who gave their all in the service of this nation. Asa and Catherine McKinley, Felix Marshall, Mary Dale Galloway, and others whom you knew and loved. Some of them are still living and here among us." This would have been the ideal moment to recognize Louisa Booth, but he could see her still contesting with the young women beside her. He decided against it.

"In today's passage from the Psalms, the true source of all of these blessings is clear: it is the Lord's work, not our own, so that none may boast. Human effort and accomplishment may be acts of obedience, but they avail nothing without the power and mercy of God. 'The eyes of all look to thee, O Lord; thou givest them their meat in due season; thou openest thine hand, and satisfiest the desire of every living thing.'"

He could see now that Louisa was pawing at her clothing, handling the small buttons at the collar of her old-fashioned pinstriped blouse. She managed to open them, exposing her throat; then, with effort, she pulled the tucked-in blouse away from her gored skirt. Her hands continued to unbutton the blouse.

"Likewise, the passage from the second book of Kings involves the Prophet Elisha dealing with a famine in the land. About a hundred men are assembled in the company of prophets, and Elisha has nothing to feed them. Someone creates a stew from the gourds of a wild vine, and it proves to be poisonous. Yet the Lord transforms the stew into a wholesome food, and they all share it. Then, a farmer presents a small gift of barley loaves and some ears of grain. Far too little to feed the crowd. Yet Elisha commands, 'Give it to the people, that they may eat.' And indeed they did, and there was bread left over. The Lord it was who multiplied and purified the little they gave, until it supplied them all."

David continued, but with his eyes now glued on Louisa Booth, who had opened all of the buttons of her blouse. To his horror, he now saw her take off the blouse and toss it to the floor. People nearby had become aware of what was happening and looked with wide eyes at Louisa sitting there in her undergarments. David asked himself what he should do. With a rising sense of alarm, he went on with the sermon, trying to pull everyone's attention away from the situation in the pews.

"Today's Gospel passage finds Jesus in a similar position. He has gone away by boat to a remote spot, seeking solitude. Instead he finds a massive crowd, over five thousand men and their families. Many are sick, and he climbs out of the boat to move among them, healing and comforting them. 'He saw a great multitude, and he was moved with compassion toward them, and he healed their sick.' When evening came, they were still there, and had nothing to eat. His disciples produced five loaves of bread and two fish. How could these meet the need of the multitude? But Jesus accepted them . . . he looked up to heaven, blessed the food, broke it into pieces, and gave it to the disciples, who distributed it among the people."

Louisa was now working at the metal hooks holding together the corset around her body. It was a relic of an earlier day, reaching from the bustline to the waist, stiffened by whalebone stays. The hooks were rather large and fitted into eyes, not easily detached. But she had been wearing this outmoded style for years, rejecting the permissive clothing of the 1920s. She had fastened and unfastened that corset countless times and knew how it was done. With a gesture of disgust, she wrenched it off and threw it to the floor. There was a small gasp from those seated around her.

"The people in these stories provided only the most flawed and inadequate gifts, nowhere near what was actually needed. Yet the Lord accepted them, blessed them, sanctified them, and multiplied them. Even a pot of poisonous stew was cleansed, then fed to many. In both stories, there is such an abundance created that a surfeit of food was left over after they had eaten and been satisfied. Whatever we bring to the Lord in obedience, he will multiply. He will purify, he will employ to enact his great purpose. He asks only that we give what we have, and allow him to transform it into what is needful."

The final garment was a camisole of light cotton batiste, held together with ribbons. These were very easy to untie. Louisa stripped off the camisole and was now entirely naked above the waist. Instead of tossing it away, she used the camisole as a towel to mop the perspiration from her skin. Pushing up each ample breast, she wiped the sweat from the crease underneath it. Louisa was a solid block of a woman, broad-shouldered and long-limbed. Not easily tractable by physical means or by persuasion. It was now clear to nearly everyone in the church that an incident of an unprecedented nature was going on.

Chapter 10

A child giggled, and a quick slap put a stop to that at once. There was an overwhelming wave of painful embarrassment. But every adult in the room was aware of Miss Booth's heroic service during the dreadful years of war and deportation, and—despite her imperious and often condescending manner—they would not allow her to be mocked.

As David watched it unfold, he felt another pervasive emotion in the room as well: empathy. The Buraani Christians all around were flooding her with a tender comprehension, a sense that they understood what it was to be helpless against a strong influence—the power of the ruler, the landlord, the soldier, the patriarch, the employer, the master; the tyranny of anguish, poverty, illness, and loss. She was in thrall to her dementia, and somehow they felt it with her. In the innocence of her deteriorating mind, she had made herself more comfortable in the stifling heat. There was no manifestation among the people of any desire to condemn. In fact, probably many wished they could do the same thing.

"There is a greater level of interpretation opened up in today's Gospel reading. When was another time that Jesus took bread, lifted it up, blessed it, broke it and gave it to his disciples? Yes, it was at the final supper he shared with them, just before his arrest, his trial, his crucifixion. And what did he say to them that evening? 'Take and eat, this is my body, which is broken for you.' Jesus himself gave his ultimate gift, his own life, to the Lord, and it was used to feed us, not merely with a single meal but as the spiritual food that provides us with eternal life."

David leaned into the pulpit and raised his voice a little. "The Lord knows how weak we are, how flawed. He has nothing but compassion on our illness, our hunger, our failure, our need. All of us in this room have known hunger and sickness and violence, especially in the past ten years. Many of us have suffered terrible losses. We are together in this need, all of one body in our pain. On this earth we pass through trial. We go without . . . and sometimes even what we have is taken from us. But this saying is true and worthy of full acceptance: that Christ Jesus came into the world to save us, to feed us, to heal us. Thanks be to God."

"Amen!" exclaimed the people, with heartfelt relief.

Everyone rose for the closing hymn, and Louisa Booth chose that moment to depart. With difficulty she stood, and turned toward the doors; her helpers scrambled to pick up the discarded clothing, and to accompany her out of the church. With an awkward dignity she hobbled down the aisle on her two crutches, still shockingly topless. Some faces turned away, blushing, but many looked towards her, with expressions of compassion and concern. Whether she noted them at all is unknown.

David offered the closing prayer. "O God, the Protector of all who trust in thee, without whom nothing is strong, nothing is holy: increase and multiply upon us thy mercy, that we may pass through things temporal, and finally lose not the things eternal. Grant this, O heavenly Father, for Jesus' sake. Amen."

With both hands raised, David added, "The grace of the Lord Jesus Christ, and the love of God, and the communion of the Holy Ghost, be with us all. Amen."

The congregation of the Adamu church never departed quickly, as they were keen to mingle and visit with each other, and many wanted to speak to one of the pastors for various reasons. David took his place near the door and greeted each of them on their way out. By the time the crowd thinned, he was ready to drop from tension, heat and fatigue. But suddenly he remembered his promise to meet with Shueyda Momonen after the service. Slowly, he made his way toward the pastor's office.

He found Shueyda patiently reading his Bible and waiting. "Do you know, Brother David . . . I have just noticed something about the passage from Matthew you preached from today. Chapter fourteen begins not with Jesus, but with John the Baptist. John has offended Herod the king, and Herod puts him to death. John's disciples have just buried him, and then they told Jesus. And that is why Jesus withdraws to a place apart."

David was hanging up his pulpit robe, mopping his face, and not listening as attentively as he should have. Shueyda continued, "So, Jesus is mourning the death of his cousin John, desiring to be alone . . . but instead, he must deal with a great crowd of people all demanding his help. He spends the whole day with them, and then finally, after all of this, he goes up upon a mountain to pray." Shueyda's eyes were shining. "That night, he rescues his disciples on a boat in the storm. And as soon as they reach Gennesaret, another crowd collects around him there."

"Indeed . . ."

Chapter 10

"Well, you see, Jesus poured himself out for the people. Not only on the Cross, but *every day*, like a cup of water on the dry earth . . . immediately it is sucked away. There is never enough. Yet he never stops giving himself to them."

"A keen observation. I am glad that you are able to derive so much from the context."

"I am only just learning to do this. The depth of Scripture never ends."

"Thank you, Brother Shueyda. Now, about the Wednesday services . . ."

"Yes . . . I am very sorry to tell you that I cannot assist on that day."

David tried not to sigh audibly at this. He knew what was coming. "But you see, that is the day of the dedication of the new Hardy College campus," he said. "In the morning there will be a service of Holy Communion for the Christian body, a gala luncheon, and then in the afternoon the assembly of the whole school, with all of the important visitors, officials, and diplomats. We could really use your help to carry it out."

"I know. It is very unfortunate. But I must leave at once on itineration."

David valued this young man above any other; it was David who had insisted to the American members of Presbytery years ago that Shueyda was ready to be ordained and join them as a peer and a colleague, after the remarkable conversion of the village of Peshtaran.

Shueyda had proved himself an effective evangelist—not just persuading, but baptizing. Not just baptizing, but discipling, teaching new believers how to follow the faith, how to live after the model of Jesus. He trained lay leaders in each village, setting the community on a firm path. The one thing he could not achieve was to be their pastor.

He could not marry himself to a single congregation, and, forsaking all others, faithfully live out their lives together. After a while, into his heart came the call to move on to new uncharted places, and Shueyda disappeared.

That is why Shueyda was still serving as the assistant pastor at the Adamu church, because David understood this, and he was able to accept and adapt to Shueyda's many unexpected absences without a crisis. The sole pastor of a congregation could not simply take off for months or even a year or longer, with no one to cover for him. This way, the young man's extraordinary calling could be fulfilled, and David absorbed the consequences. And another young man was trained to be the pastor of the church at Peshtaran.

"Reverend Whittaker will still be here, and also Reverend Curtis Means from Aintab," the young man said. "And the pastor of the Evangelical church in Beirut—I have forgotten his name—"

"Hammond. Yes, he is expected tomorrow."

"So perhaps they can assist. Again, I apologize."

"No, you have nothing to apologize for. You must follow where the Lord leads."

"Thank you, Brother David. God bless you."

"And you. Go with my greatest affection and goodwill. And do try not to get yourself into any trouble."

Shueyda should have replied at that point with an expression of reassurance . . . but he did not. His face became very serious and still. "Goodbye, Brother David. And thank you for everything you have done for me."

"Safe journeys, my friend." Shueyda quietly got up, bowed respectfully, and left.

Galloway had a few hours to go back to his rooms in the Mission office, have a bite to eat, a wash, and a change of clothes. He drank glass after glass of pomegranate juice to replace the fluids lost. He even risked a quick nap in his armchair, and managed to wake up after a reasonable interval, with enough time to get himself over to the Windsor Hotel to await the arrival of Suzanna Hardy.

His dear friend Suzanna, chief supporter of the American Mission in Buraan for so many years. Of course she was coming for the dedication of the new Hardy College campus! Her husband, John Campbell Hardy, gone to his heavenly reward, had obligingly left her an enormous fortune derived from the steel industry in Pittsburgh. She was now a brilliant and beautiful widow in her late thirties, but not only that. She was also a sincere, knowledgeable and experienced sponsor of the missions of the United Presbyterian Church of North America, and spent a great deal of her time traveling the world to inspect and endorse their installations and outreach, however remote.

Chapter 10

During the Great War, she was unable to travel in her usual way, so she devoted herself to raising funds in the Pittsburgh area to support world missions and relief, using her charm among all of the members of corporate boards and directors of cultural organizations who populated her social strata, to propel their money where she wanted it to go. In those days, charitable giving for the institutional church was expected of such people. It was a way for the robber barons of that unbridled era to launder their wealth in a respectable manner. She had no illusions about the process.

But as soon as the war was over, she was on the sea again, in the newly launched luxury vessels designed for passengers of her class. Her faithful factotum, Mr. Gordon, had retired, but she still traveled with her lady's maid Odine, and a miniature Mr. Gordon, known as Mr. Dean. Dean was a small man, but very shrewd indeed, and as David had discovered on one of her journeys, he always traveled well armed. They came to Buraan about once a year now.

Galloway waited with increasing excitement in the nicely appointed lobby of the hotel, while uniformed staff brought him tea in a bone-china cup without being asked.

A little after five o'clock, there was a slight commotion and a sparkle of laughter at the top of the grand staircase, and David knew she had arrived. She swept quickly down the stairs, smiling, with a lady in a dark suit whom David did not know. He had eyes only for Suzanna. She wore a sleek tea-length dress of fluid silk crêpe de chine, in a glossy deep rose color . . . a matching cloche hat dressed with a sculpted rose, its petals frosted with an edge of glistening beads . . . earrings and a necklace of fine pearls, suitable for daytime. All of Suzanna's clothes were handmade for her in Paris, with the cunning details that indicate top quality.

As usual, David perceived none of these parts, only their sum: an image of feminine beauty that quite overwhelmed him.

"Oh David, my dear, there you are," she said smoothly. "Madame Marcuse, allow me to introduce my dear friend Reverend David Galloway. David, this is Henriette Marcuse."

"A great pleasure, Madame," he said.

"Henriette is staying in the rooms just across the hall. Isn't that grand? We were just talking dressmakers, sorry it won't interest you."

"Please excuse me," said the lady. "*Au revoir, mon amie.*"

"Be seeing you. Have a lovely evening," said Suzanna. The lady moved away, and Suzanna took him firmly by the hand. "You must get me out of here," she whispered. "The last thing I want to do is prattle on about clothing with a random French lady. We should go over to the new College at once."

"Now? You're ready for that?"

"Of course I am. We need to take the engineers over there so they can start unloading their equipment."

"I beg your pardon?"

"Oh David, perhaps I didn't explain. I have brought your bell, and a team to install it. They are waiting with trucks full of lumber and tools and things. If they unload the trucks tonight, they can start building a scaffold first thing tomorrow."

David's mind was spinning at this news. He latched on to the single detail he felt qualified to have an opinion about.

"Suzanna, today is the Sabbath. It's not possible for them to do that work today."

Her face looked surprised, then abashed. "Oh dear, I hadn't thought of that. When you're traveling, one day of the week tends to fade into another, I regret to say. I didn't realize it was Sunday."

"I am so sorry. What . . . what can we do about it?"

"Well, first I'll introduce you to the engineers. Then perhaps we could take them over to the campus just to have a look at the structural challenge they are facing. Perhaps then, they can make an early start tomorrow and get the bell installed in a day."

"I think that would be appropriate."

"Oh, very well then. Come along, they're in the courtyard behind the hotel." As they hurried along, Suzanna said, "I must have failed to let you know about this wonderful bell—it's just what you need for the main classroom building. A beautiful thing. Gift of the First Presbyterian Church in Pittsburgh, inscribed and everything. Wait till you see it!"

Waiting in the courtyard, smoking in the shade, were two men in canvas suits, with a number of laborers. They all got up when they spotted Suzanna.

Chapter 10

"Reverend Galloway, these are my American engineers—Mr. Brinkwater, and Mr. Hooley."

"How do you do, sir," said one, extending his hand, "Hooley, and Brinkwater."

The basic outlines of the project at hand were discussed, and Galloway asked for a car to take the four of them over to the College. All of the equipment—packed into two large trucks—was left in the courtyard under the care of the rest of the team.

As they pulled into the College grounds, Suzanna beamed with delight. "Oh, everything looks marvelous!" she said. "Such a splendid job you've done! Better than Assiut College," she added, with a little nudge. "We've done it at last."

"Without you, there would be nothing here but a stone wall around the perimeter."

"Ah, we've worked together then, have we not?" Turning to the engineers, she said, "So, what do you think, gentlemen? That's where the bell needs to go." In the center of the new administration and classroom building, a tower rose to the height of a fourth story. Hooley and Brinkwater—or, Brinkwater and Hooley, depending upon which of them one was speaking to—carefully inspected the ground all around the building, disappeared inside for a long period of time, and measured everything from the steps to the windows, jotting down notes as they went.

Galloway took Suzanna into his office, and once the doors were closed, he wrapped her in his arms and simply held her, relishing her lovely scent, the softness of her curly hair, the pliancy of her body. They had only a moment, but it was a moment to live for.

"Thank you," he whispered.

"Just you wait, my dear. There is more to come." She teased him with her gleaming eyes, and they went outside to join the engineers.

Chapter 11

Brinkwater and Hooley were on the job first thing Monday morning, as promised. Their men unloaded ranks of heavy lumber in certain pre-cut sizes and arranged them on the ground in front of the classroom building, like organ pipes. After breakfast, the resident boys were allowed to form up into an audience and watch these fascinating events.

The lowest level of a sturdy scaffold took shape quickly, then the next level. It was obvious that Hooley and Brinkwater had undertaken such a task many times before. When the wooden frame of the scaffold stood at its full height, a complex pulley system of steel cables was installed inside it, which required the rest of the morning. The assistant math and science master, Mr. Barburi, explained each step to the rapt audience. It was a teachable moment.

David Galloway stayed in his office all morning, but Mr. Flynn did not appear. He had been directed to present himself on Monday at nine o'clock to discuss the uproar at the Rileys' dinner party on Saturday night, including a formal summons in writing delivered to his home. David was not keen to call him on the carpet for his aggressive outburst. But he needed to make it clear that Flynn's attack upon poor Dr. Dillon and his fiancée was not acceptable, and—if it could possibly be done—to reconcile Mr. Flynn to the community.

David had to admit he felt relieved that Harris Flynn had decided to refuse an interview. David was free now to interpret Flynn's act as a resignation, to document the incident, and to report it to the UPNA. However, David also had to record it in his own mind as another personal failure.

Chapter 11

Also, he needed to tell Mr. Barburi that he suddenly had two more classes to teach that semester. But the science master was getting a nice promotion to go with them.

After the noon meal, it might have been nice to take it easy during the hottest part of the day. Instead, the work resumed with steady determination. The lift system they installed upon the wooden scaffold proved to be a block and tackle consisting of pairs of pulleys joined by the steel cables, which excited Mr. Barburi to no end, as he explained to the boys how this arrangement multiplied the mechanical advantage.

Soon it was time to move the bell into position. A sizable wooden crate emerged slowly from one of the trucks on a wheeled platform. They had constructed a ramp to roll it from the truck to the ground, and then a few meters to the base of the scaffold. At that point they uncrated it, and the beauty of the bell was fully revealed.

It was not simply a bell, of course, but a complete assembly consisting of the yoke, the rotary wheel, and the cast-iron side mountings and undercarriage, holding the bell in a sort of cage-like housing in which it could swing. The bell itself was about twenty-four inches in diameter and the entire unit weighed nearly three hundred pounds. The solid bronze was cast in a single piece, then finished with a hanging clapper. Its burnished surface gleamed in the sun. The boys were allowed to come close to it, see it and even touch it, and on the resonator they could read the engraved inscription: *Dedicated to the Glory of God on the Ninth of September 1925 Gift of the First Presbyterian Church of Pittsburgh Pennsylvania to the Church of Jesus Christ in Buraan*. Across the cast-iron yoke, raised letters spelled out *Mercer and Company Bellfoundry Pittsburgh Penn*. It was a most impressive object and the boys' hearts swelled with pride at the thought that it would adorn their very own school.

While all of this admiration was taking place, the work crew set up a gasoline motor and a winch. The boys were moved to a safe distance while the cables were attached to the mountings and the lift of the winch tested. Mr. Barburi explained how the gasoline motor turned the cylinder and shortened the cable, raising the bell's weight. At last they were ready, and the lift commenced.

Slowly, the bell assembly was raised to the height of the first story of the classroom building, and the men slid braces of lumber underneath it like a temporary floor. Tension on the cable eased while the crew made safety checks. Then, they cranked the winch again, and the bell rose bit by bit to the second story. Again they braced it. Step by step, the bell climbed the scaffold, gradually reaching the fourth story, right beside the bell tower.

Reaching from the scaffold into the tower they had built a horizontal arm, like a crane, with a set of steel rollers on which the bell could ride into place. Inch by inch, the cables moved the bell across this bridge and into the tower. The necks of all the boys were straining to their limits to observe this process. Mr. Barburi produced some field glasses through which he watched and then narrated aloud to them, like a sportscaster.

Some members of the team were already in the tower, ready for the bell's arrival. When at length it settled into position, they waved their arms to signal success, and there was an outburst of cheering from the crowd. The team carefully bolted the bell assembly to the tower structure, then released the cable and began to install the bellrope.

It was now late in the afternoon and the boys were obliged to wash and dress, go to chapel, and to supper. The work crew would need to dismantle the scaffold on the following day. Satisfied with their progress, they decided it was time to go back to the Windsor Hotel with their gear, and then off to the nearest local for a well-earned pint.

That same evening found Shueyda Momonen in a humble tea-stall in Charga, just outside the capital city of Buraan. Dameotis was the active business and political center of the country, arranged around the working waterfront. The palace complex of the King and court occupied the upper slopes of the city, surrounded by government ministries and the newer Europeanized district of Hosna, where the expatriate and diplomatic community lived.

Shueyda had not departed immediately after church on Sunday. He had spent the rest of the day in fasting and prayer, preparing himself to travel. Monday morning he left, on his old black bicycle, with a small bag containing his Bible, a little food and a change of clothes. It would take him all day to get to Charga if he managed to hitchhike part of the way on a passing truck or commercial vehicle. Drivers often picked up travelers along the

Chapter 11

road, grateful for some conversation and company. And in Buraan, almost all roads led to the capital, as to Rome.

Above Dameotis, a ridge of rocky cliffs bordered the city, and just beyond that was the dry inland plateau. This was barren and ascetic country, bumpy with rocks and few knots of gray scrub, like the salt flats of Utah or the natron wastes of monastic Egypt. And it was here that the Hanamid cult center of Charga had ruled its little world since ancient times.

Charga thrived on a single industry: the immolation of Buraani dead. Through fire the believer was united with the divine, the sun god Tavus, and delivered from the earthly and material Tavibus. The symbolism was perfect for their dualistic and gnostic belief system. And there was no better place to die and be cremated than the holy city of Charga.

Shueyda lingered at the table over his glass of tea and a small cheese sandwich, even though a knot of rough-looking men smoked and played a game of dice beside him. He needed to speak to the proprietor. He seized a moment when the man was sitting on a crate and having his own tea break.

"Good evening, sir. Grace and peace to you."

The man looked at him skeptically. "What do you want?"

"Can you please tell me if there is any lodging available nearby?"

The man frowned and scratched his stubbly beard. "This town is stuffed like a bitch with ten pups. All the short-timers are here waiting for their chance to burn. Everybody wants to go during the holidays." It was the holy month of Shahreel and the merit of cremation at this time of year rose proportionally.

"I don't need much . . . just a room."

"There's usually a place at the Veegos'. Go down the alley that way to the end, and then ask again. You'll find it."

"Thank you. God bless you." The man scowled at him as if he had said something quite offensive.

Shueyda pushed his bicycle slowly through the overcrowded alleyways, asking directions as politely as he knew how. He often got the same rude treatment. He finally came to a square cinder-block house with a muddy yard in front where someone had been doing laundry. Cotton towels hung on a clothesline. Stepping carefully, he made his way to the door and called out, "Hello? Is anyone home?"

The face of a child perhaps ten years old appeared at the open window. "Mama! Somebody's here."

A woman of about thirty opened the door. She looked tired, but not hostile. "Good evening . . . can I help you?"

"Blessings upon your house, madam. I would like to find a room for tonight."

"Well . . . we don't have a room, exactly. But you could stay up there," she said, gesturing toward the roof. Built into the outer wall of the house was a flight of stairs. She led the way to the flat dusty roof, where a canvas shelter stood above a wooden cot. "I'll bring you some water and a blanket. You'd better carry your bike up here, too—you don't want to leave it near the street. Four *tomaans*, payable in advance."

"Here you are. Four *tomaans*."

"Sorry, but we have had our supper already. I won't have any food in the house until I get to the market tomorrow."

"I have eaten. Thank you."

She brought him the water, a blanket and two clean towels. He folded up one of them and used it as a pillow. As soon as full darkness fell, the densely populated neighborhood became surprisingly quiet, and Shueyda slept.

He was alerted in the morning by his host coming back into the dooryard with bundles from the market. She called up to him. "I've got enough to make some breakfast here, if you want to come down."

This time he was accepted into the simple *salaamlek* of the house, where a table was set for three. To his surprise, the family intended to eat with him. "Breakfast is extra," she said, busy with preparation. "Two *tomaans*." He placed the two coins upon the table.

She laid out a substantial meal for them, with fresh bread, boiled eggs, yogurt, tart cherry compote, and an array of sliced cucumbers and tomatoes. Definitely worth two *tomaans*. As they sat down, Shueyda held up his hands and prayed. "Father of all mercies, I give thanks for a safe arrival, and for this bountiful food provided by thy hand. Bless this house and all who dwell herein. In the name of Jesus Christ our Lord, amen." The woman and her child stared at him but said nothing about it.

"Here, help yourself. I'm Jadali Veego, and this is my son Arrun."

Chapter 11

"Honored to know you. My name is Shueyda Momonen . . . I'm from Adamu."

She shot him an unsmiling glance. "How did you know to come here, to our house?"

"I asked about . . . people in the tea shop and the street."

"Yes, they all know the Veego house, inn of last resort. The holy people won't stay here. Since my husband was killed at the quarry and I took them to court. It's a deathtrap of course, that quarry, but unless you are a priest it's the only employer in this district, for poor people anyway. They don't want anyone calling them on it, how dangerous the work is there, and how the managers don't care if you die."

Her eyes flashed with anger. "My husband Arrun spent every week there, in those shithole dormitories, working from daybreak till dark. He came home for a day, then started again. Making blocks with sand and ashes and rock dust. It wore him away like a dry bone. There was nothing left of him. And then one day there was another accident and he died there."

"I am so very sorry for your loss, Mrs. Veego."

"That makes one person in this town. I filed a wrongful death suit against them . . . it's now in the Court of Cassation. It will be there forever and I'll never see a single *tomaan* from it, I know that. But I couldn't let them do that to my husband and just take it."

The words poured out, drawn by a listening ear. "You're not allowed to question the powers that be. Not the priests, not the quarry company, not the government people. They spread the rumor that this is a foul house because a woman takes in lodgers with no man living here. Well, if they hadn't killed my husband he would be here, wouldn't he? But none of these pilgrims coming here to die want to take a chance on their holiness by lodging with an immoral woman. I guess they want me to give up and leave town. But this house is all I've got."

"Why don't the priests help you? A widow in need?"

She laughed bitterly. "Perhaps you have just arrived in this world from beyond the stars. The priests don't care about us. They care only about the rich and their big donations. They care about the cremation fees." A cynical public was the inevitable result of excessive clericalism.

"In the Holy Bible it is written that pure and undefiled religion is this: to assist the fatherless and widows in their affliction, and to keep oneself from the evil of the world. And Jesus himself scorned the holy people who wear long robes, and love to be greeted with respect in the city, and have the best seats at wedding feasts, but devour widows' houses and then for show make long prayers."

Jadali stared at him, with annoyance this time. "I don't understand what you are saying. You talk like a priest, and yet like the opposite of a priest."

Shueyda held her eyes for long moment. "I am a follower of Jesus. That's all."

"Whatever you say," she replied dismissively. "I've got things to do."

Shueyda spent most of that day walking all over Charga, orienting himself. He located the various open markets, the shopping streets, the trades and services, the ubiquitous guest-houses for dying pilgrims and their kin. As he expected, he found no churches, not even a Catholic or Orthodox one.

On the edge of the city stood a long featureless wall of earthen brick, broken only by a narrow gate. It surrounded an enclosure of great antiquity, open to the sky. A colonnade around the edge offered the only shelter from the noonday sun. Within that shaded area were spread many large old carpets. Groups of kinfolk had gathered and were sitting on the rugs, waiting for the daily ceremony to start.

In the open space in the center of the large courtyard stood several rows of stone altars or biers. On each of these altars was placed a large mummy-like parcel, wrapped in white. Each bundle lay saturated in ghee mixed with alcohol.

When the sun reached its zenith, someone appeared bearing a huge heavy sistrum and shaking it fiercely. Its saucer-sized polished brass disks glinted in the sun and made a chiming sound like a dozen little pairs of cymbals. All those seated rose. A portly man in a slate-blue cassock and turban led a procession of similarly-dressed assistants, who took their places at each altar, holding flaming torches. At a signal from the leader, all of the people tipped back their heads and raised their hands, and prayed

Chapter 11

aloud in unison, an undulating current of prayer, flowing and lapping in murmured tones.

A young assistant walked out toward the center of the enclosure carrying a great golden bowl from which the chief priest drew a long wand with a perforated globe on the end, like a large tea-ball. He went from altar to altar, sprinkling each bundle with a clear fluid, as the voices rippled on and on.

As the prayer came to an end, the leader added a few words, and the priest at each altar reached out with his burning torch to ignite the fire. There was a rush of flame and billowing smoke as the priests retreated and the fuel wrapped in the white dressings quickly caught and burned. The chief priest walked away casually . . . all in a day's work.

The families sat down again to wait for the process to take its course, while Shueyda quietly departed.

That afternoon when the shops reopened and foot traffic increased, he went to the outdoor market and bought a few things. From a melon seller he bought a sturdy wooden crate. And at a fish stall, he bought a tin pail, and asked them to wash it out for him.

He set down the crate on the edge of the main square, where there was some open space, and climbed up on it like a pedestal. He then pulled out a little wooden wind instrument and started to play. In only a few minutes a group of listeners collected, smiling and nodding. Then he used the upturned bucket as a drum and began to beat out rhythms with his hands, and sing.

He chose many of the simple, singable gospel tunes enjoyed every week by the congregation in Adamu, songs from David Galloway's Shenandoah boyhood, translated into basic Buraani verses. The call-and-response pattern was very easy to learn, as the leader offered one new line in each verse, then a chorus everyone could repeat. One little song could go on indefinitely, as someone improvised a new guiding line.

"I'm going to sit at the welcome table . . . I'm going to sit at the welcome table one of these days—hallelujah! I'm going to feast on milk and honey, feast on milk and honey one of these days!"

Standing on the crate, drumming on the pail, he soon had a willing choir of voices before him, singing with great pleasure. Soon he got them rocking as they sang, "I'm leaning, leaning, leaning on the everlasting arms..."

From the crowd, Shueyda picked out a young boy with a lovely voice and brought him forward, coaching him to help lead the song. "What a fellowship, what a joy divine, what a blessedness, what a peace is mine, safe and secure from all alarms! Oh how sweet to walk in this pilgrim way, oh how bright the path grows from day to day, leaning on the everlasting arms!"

The music went on for about an hour, as more passersby joined the crowd and others left. He drew on a stock of common Buraani folk songs, modified to deliver Christian content, but still universal in their appeal. He ended with a bouncing crowd favorite, "I've got a home in glory land that outshines the sun... I've got a home in glory land that outshines the sun..." He scanned the faces to judge whether anyone picked up the subtle message. Finally, he sang, "I took Jesus as my Saviour, you take him too! I took Jesus as my Saviour, you take him too! While he's calling you!"

Even at this, the people were too involved in the music to react. But he thought he saw some frowning faces at the edge of the crowd, a cluster of young men, standing apart.

When Shueyda got back to his space on the roof at the Veego house that evening, he found that it had received an upgrade. On the wooden bedstead there was a cotton mattress, stuffed with fleece. A soft woolen rug was spread upon the floor. A candle in a small brass holder and a penny packet of matches stood on a crate beside the bed.

He lighted the candle and sat on the rug, reading his Bible. After a little while, a voice floated up the stairs. "Hello? May I come up? I've got something for you."

"Of course, Mrs. Veego."

She appeared with a tray, bearing two glasses of lemon hibiscus tea. "You could call me Jadali. No one here ever does." She placed the tray in the middle of the rug and sat down on the other end of it, facing him. "I saw you in the market today. I didn't know you were a musician."

"I'm not. I'm an evangelist."

"So... what does that mean?"

"It means I go from place to place, telling people about Jesus."

Chapter 11

She shook her head. "You've got to be crazy, then. Why would you come here? This is the priests' town. Everybody here belongs to the fire temple. They don't want to hear about your Jesus."

"I come here because I love Jesus. And because Jesus loves everyone who lives here."

"Ohhh, Shueyda," she sighed. "You're such a nice man, but you don't make any sense."

They drank their tea and talked some more, as the darkness deepened, with the easy intimacy that comes with candlelight and stars. She took the tea things away, and Shueyda made her accept another four *tomaans*. He then spent a long time in prayer.

On the following day, Shueyda came to the open market at about the same hour. There were people actually waiting for him, hoping for another songfest. He did not disappoint them. A large crowd quickly formed. Their ability to learn songs with little effort and their evident joy in performing them were his great allies in this mission.

Several people looked around for a hat or a bowl in which to offer coins, but this street entertainer was collecting no money. It seemed he made music for the pleasure of it.

After about thirty minutes of singing, Shueyda addressed the crowd. "People of Charga," he began, "I perceive that you are very religious. So religious are you, in fact, that you worship both the source of good and the source of evil, two gods, without distinction. The sun god and the earth god . . . of the spiritual and the material realms. And I must say, in many ways, that is a smart policy."

A few people walked away, but many remained. "If you understand worship to be the appeasement of a powerful authority, then you want to satisfy them equally and so earn their approval and avert their wrath. But *our* God, the *one* God who made the universe and everything in it and called it good, is not like an earthly ruler, flawed and fallible, acting on impulse, yielding to flattery or acts of sacrifice. No! Our God cares only for justice, and the one true faith."

A murmur passed through the crowd. "Moreover, our God regards his people with love and mercy, even when they resist or reject him. Indeed, while we were yet far from him, he reached out to us with his grace and forgiveness, sending to us his son Jesus to take on our mortal life and overcome the power of sin and death. This is the God we serve, and our worship is not a craven appeasement but rather a response in love to him who first loved us. We offer him our thanks and praise and receive his blessings, not as mere vassals but as beloved sons and daughters, at peace with our heavenly Father. That is the good news of Jesus Christ that I bring to you today.

"My friends," he continued, "How can I sing so confidently of my future home in heaven? Because Jesus promised it to us. And God demonstrated the truth of his word by raising Jesus from death to life. Jesus was killed by wicked men, but God raised him up again. And this powerful life is now offered to us as the free gift of God in Christ.

"How do we gain this wonderful life for ourselves? Do we earn it through meritorious works? No, not at all. If we could earn it, God's free gift would mean nothing. No, God offers it through his loving grace to anyone who believes in his Son, Jesus."

The crowd was actually more numerous now, as the curious stopped to hear what he was saying. "Why then do Christians so often show a vast change in their behavior when they come to believe in Jesus? Why do they stop getting drunk, cheating on their wives, beating their children? Why do they go to church willingly, give to help the poor, and sing God's praises with joy? Are they earning merit with God? No! They are expressing the happiness they have found and responding to God's love with their love. That is the essence of the Christian life, my friends."

Shueyda thought he spotted the group of young men from yesterday, forming up on the edge of the crowd. Their faces were angry and they were shuffling forward, getting closer to him.

"So do not listen to those who say that you must placate the wrath of the gods or buy the favor of the gods by repeating rituals or giving money to the priests. Only call on the name of Jesus, and you will be saved."

At this point, a rock flew out of the crowd and hit the wall behind him. Another quickly followed, and this one hit Shueyda in the face, splitting his lip. The crowd reacted with shock and dismay, and turned on the young men throwing stones, scolding them. Stunned, he sat down on the crate, and blood flowed from his mouth onto his white tunic and trousers. In the

Chapter 11

general disorder that followed, a few people came toward him to help. One of them was Jadali Veego.

Jadali and a few music lovers helped Shueyda to his feet, picked up his crate and his bucket, and took him home.

The next day, she caught him coming down the stairs outside her house with his crate and bucket, preparing to go back to the marketplace.

Jadali was furious. "What am I supposed to do with you?" she snapped. "You're like a little child who just doesn't think. You can't go back there—you can barely talk through that nasty lip. You're lucky you still have all of your teeth. I'm saying right now, you are not going back there today!"

She blocked the stairs down to the yard, planting her body in his path. "The people in the square, they love your music. Why would you say all of those crazy things to them? Are you out of your mind? Are you trying to get yourself beat up or killed? I told you, everyone in Charga lives off of the priests and their business. They are not going to let you mess that up. I can't believe I have to explain this to a grown man. I guess it's because you're not from around here."

Shueyda attempted a reply, but she was right—his swollen lip muffled his words.

"There, you see? Who is going to listen to you like that?" Her tone changed. "Please . . . please don't go there today. Just go back up those stairs and keep to yourself for a little while. I'll bring you anything you need."

She was as good as her word, and better . . . she kept finding reasons to come up the stairs and bring him something. She dabbed a little almond oil on his wound to help it heal.

On the following day, his split lip was improved, and Jadali knew she had no power to keep him away from the marketplace. That afternoon he carried his things back to the same spot and again found a crowd of music fans waiting for him. He went through all of their favorites from previous days and taught them a few more challenging songs. His little apprentice showed up again and sang like a star. At times Shueyda could accompany them on the wooden flute while the people carried the melody and a volunteer drummed on the tin pail.

Finally, he moved into concert mode and sang for them, a long recitation of the ballads that told Bible stories in the style of their own religious music. The Hanamid faith was chiefly an oral tradition, relying upon the repetition of metaphysical chants known as the *Qasidas*. The church in Adamu had adapted this familiar style, plaintive and discursive, for teaching narratives from the life of Jesus.

It was a risky tactic to deliver new content in the style of their own holy psalms and songs. But the crowd seemed to absorb it easily.

He chose stories that illustrated the loving nature of God: the lilies of the field, the birds of the air, and how their Heavenly Father provides for them.

He sang about the sower who spreads seeds on rocky soil, on the open path where it quickly disappears, on shallow soil where it springs up but dies without deep roots, and finally on rich and receptive soil, where it grows and brings forth abundant grain.

He sang about the Good Samaritan, an outcaste who came upon a traveler lying wounded by the side of the road. The priests saw the wounded man but did nothing to help. But the outcaste rescued him, treated his wounds and took him to a shelter for care.

He sang about the Prodigal Son, who rejected his father, took his father's money and ran off, and later was forced to come home in shame and need. His father never rejected him in turn, but ran out and welcomed him, rejoicing that his son had returned, forgiving his offenses, and bringing him back into the family.

And Shueyda sang about the ultimate act of love: Jesus losing his own life to the harsh powers of empire and temple. Jesus giving his own body and blood to reconcile errant humanity to God. It was moving, captivating music and storytelling, and the crowd was drawn into it; there were tears on many faces.

And then without warning two police trucks thrust themselves into the market square. The crowd was thrown into confusion as officers spilled out of the trucks and began beating them with fists and clubs. They seemed to be arresting people at random. Before Shueyda could react, they pulled him down from the crate and shoved him to the ground face down, where one of the police pinned him with his weight on Shueyda's back, between the shoulder blades. An officer stood on each side of him, with a heavy foot

Chapter 11

on his hands, grinding them against the ground. They held him this way, in pain, unable to take a breath, until the square was cleared.

As the officer lifted his foot from Shueyda's left hand, he gave it an extra stomp, just out of pure vindictiveness. He felt a sort of *ping* like a guitar string breaking. The officers tossed him into the back of one of their vehicles with the others and sped away.

They were taken to a holding cell at Charga's local jail, which was unfortunately already very crowded, and mostly underground. The atmosphere was airless, stinking, and the only places on the floor to sit were at the end of the room closest to the drain, which served as the toilet. The new arrivals clustered together at that end. Overcome with shock and pain, Shueyda held his left hand close against his body, shut his eyes, and withdrew inside himself.

After a while he began to look around him and recognized several of the men from the crowd who had enjoyed his music. One of them had a conspiratorial expression on his face. "You shouldn't have said those things about the King," he whispered. "That was your big mistake."

"What? What did I say about the King?"

"You know, when you said that your God is not like an earthly ruler, who must be flattered and appeased. You said he was full of faults and flaws. I was there, I heard it myself."

"That is not what I meant."

"Doesn't matter what you think you meant, you fool. We heard what you said."

The hours passed painfully into night. They were not fed. A faint light entered the room through slats at street level. Unconsciously, Shueyda began to hum a little, under his breath. After a few minutes, some of those sitting around him picked up the tune and began to hum as well. Shueyda then sang, in a very gentle, low voice.

"I am having hard trials trying to get home . . . ohhh, I'm having hard trials trying to get home . . . ohhh, I'm having hard trials, having hard trials . . . yes, I'm having hard trials trying to get home."

Before long, many of the men there, beaten down by the injustices and reversals of daily life, separated from their homes, took up the song. "I am climbing high mountains trying to get home . . . ohhh, my way's sometimes weary, trying to get home... yes, I'm bearing great burdens, bearing great burdens, Lord, I'm bearing great burdens trying to get home..."

A day or two later, several of the men, including Shueyda, were transferred to the regional detention center in Dameotis. They felt they had effectively vanished from the face of the earth.

Jadali Veego came to the Charga jail several times each day, persisting until she learned what had happened to those arrested in the market square. She raided her tiny hidden purse of emergency savings and took the money to one of the scribes who sat in certain spots around the market, reading and writing letters for the illiterate public. She carefully dictated a letter to the Jesus followers in the town Shueyda had come from, hoping that someone there would be able to step up and help him. She paid for the postage, and had the writer address it:

> *To the friends of Shueyda Momonen*
> *Jesus Church*
> *Adamu*

She kept his crate, and his pail, and his wooden flute, and his bicycle, and his small handlebar bag, and his Bible, arranging them in his room upon her roof... resolving to hold them there until he came back for them.

The letter took several weeks to reach Adamu and then circulate slowly around the various churches in town, until at last it reached David Galloway.

Chapter 12

But on that Tuesday, the eighth of September, David Galloway knew nothing of his younger colleague's venture into Charga—only that he was away and could be expected to remain incommunicado for an extended period. Galloway had accepted the fact that only Shueyda Momonen and the Holy Spirit knew where he was and what he was doing at any given point in time.

David spent most of that Tuesday making final preparations for the ceremonies and celebrations on Wednesday.

He discovered, with gratitude, that God had blessed him again in the persons of Mr. Brinkwater and Mr. Hooley, the engineers brought by Suzanna from the United States to install her lovely bell. Not only did they do a superb job in record time, so far as David could tell, but it turned out that they had a plan in their back pocket to establish themselves in Buraan with their own engineering business. There was not likely to be enough work for them in Adamu, but in the capital city of Dameotis, a great deal of building, renovating and upgrading of standards was going on, as demand expanded for amenities like electric light and indoor plumbing, and novelties such as elevators and laundry machines.

In fact, they had already incorporated their business in the country as *Hooley and Brinkwater Consulting Engineers*. Apparently, Mr. Hooley had prevailed at last. They confirmed that maintaining the power and water systems at the College and the Hospital would be no problem for them at all, and so they enlisted their first customers.

They dismantled the scaffolding and packed away all of that equipment, yet their work on campus was apparently not yet done. They were busy with a construction project at the front gate of the College, which was off limits to all, including David. Suzanna had made him swear on his honor not to pry into that project until it was complete. A wooden barrier had been installed to shield it from view. Suzanna loved to surprise him, and on the whole her surprises were thoughtful and welcome ones.

The chief business of that Tuesday was the very long and tedious meeting of the local Board of Management for Hardy College, plus those members of the Board of Oversight in the United States who were present for the opening convocation. These meetings normally took place in both Buraani and English, and involved detailed discussions of plans, problems and policies. David Galloway was a committed consensus-builder. He would work with an issue until he perceived comprehension and consent among all of the members of the Boards. Imposing his will by authority was not in his nature. He also believed that it was counter-productive, since everyone would exert themselves to implement only such policies as they understood and could agree on. He believed that the tedious meetings represented a reasonable price to pay for their cooperation.

That evening found him satisfied with their progress. There was so much achievement to be thankful for; the College in its present form was the realization of a dream long held by each member of the Boards.

But David had not enjoyed more than a moment alone with Suzanna. She had arranged for the two of them to have dinner at the Windsor Hotel in a small private dining room—well aware that he would never agree to visit her in her own suite—and it was a little oasis for him of comfort and joy. His heart was full.

The great day finally arrived, and David noted with much appreciation that the weather was far less hot and uncomfortable—a special mercy. It began with the Sacrament of the Lord's Supper, a significant occasion in the Presbyterian tradition of that era, celebrated only four or five times a year and limited to examined members of the Church. The AMB staff from all stations looked forward to sharing it together. While it was taking place in the Assembly Hall, the French master, Monsieur Chevet, a Roman Catholic, led the visitors who were not eligible for Holy Communion in the Presbyterian polity on a guided tour of the new buildings.

Chapter 12

The liturgy of the Lord's Supper was a solemn and humbling one, and included this prayer: "Most merciful God, we bless thy holy Name for all thy servants who have kept the faith, and are at rest with thee . . . " David's mind again populated the room with those who were no longer with them. Mary Dale and their daughter Anne rose before his eyes. He had asked that Mauris Agarin, the music master, prepare Galloway's favorite hymn:

> My faith looks up to thee
> Thou Lamb of Calvary
> Saviour divine
> Now hear me while I pray
> Take all my guilt away
> Oh, let me from this day
> Be wholly thine.
>
> May thy rich grace impart
> Strength to my fainting heart
> My zeal inspire
> As thou hast died for me
> Oh, may my love to thee
> Pure, warm and changeless be
> A living fire.
>
> While life's dark maze I tread
> And griefs around me spread
> Be thou my guide
> Bid darkness turn to day
> Wipe sorrow's tears away
> Nor let me ever stray
> From thee aside.
>
> When ends life's transient dream
> When death's cold sullen stream
> Shall o'er me roll
> Blest Saviour, then, in love
> Fear and distrust remove
> Oh, bear me save above
> A ransomed soul.

It might have been a mistake, since David could rarely get through that hymn without choking on tears.

After the service, Galloway warmly greeted the special guests and dignitaries who had arrived for the gala luncheon and the convocation event. The pastors of Adamu's Roman Catholic, Greek, Armenian and Syriac Orthodox churches were there, and the Education Minister from Dameotis was expected shortly. The American Ambassador to Buraan sent his regrets, as he was in Washington at the time. Many lesser municipal officials were looking forward to the festive meal.

Just as Galloway and Dr. Dillon were greeting Buraan's new Health Minister, a car drove up containing the Turkish Governor of the province, Ismail Bey. In the car were also Ismail's lovely wife, whom James Dillon had rescued in her dangerously complicated pregnancy six years ago, and their little son Iskender. The boy bounced out of the car and ran over to his pediatrician, yelling, "Doctor Dillon! Doctor Dillon!" and wrapped his arms around him. They all savored the sweetness of that encounter.

Ismail Bey explained to the Health Minister the drama surrounding Iskender's birth and the debt they owed to the American Mission and its hospital staff. The Minister regarded James Dillon with greater attention and began to ask him specific questions about the College and its medical education program. And at that opportune moment, they were joined by Dillon's fiancée Marya Olorzey and her brother Eyvor, resident physician at the American Mission Hospital and stellar graduate of the Hardy College medical school.

The refectory was festooned with ribbons and great baskets of flowers, and the luncheon represented the best that Adamu had to offer. The official guests at the high table were introduced and took the opportunity to say a few words.

Shortly before three o'clock, the audience made their way to places inside the Assembly Hall. In the courtyard outside, the faculty and students, in suitable academic gowns and nice new school uniforms, were firmly organized into queues by Mr. Tola, Galloway's office assistant. Precisely at three—punctuality being a trait they aimed to instill in the College boys—they could hear Mr. Agarin at the grand piano beginning the vigorous hymn *A Mighty Fortress Is Our God*. Well rehearsed, the boys knew exactly at what point to start singing, as they all processed through the wide-open doors into the Assembly Hall.

Chapter 12

There were words of welcome, prayers of dedication, musical performances by groups of students—including an extraordinary duet on violin and cello by two senior boys. The Minister of Education arrived just in time to present greetings and encouraging words on behalf of the King and the Buraani government. And then it was time for Galloway's convocation address.

David had been working on this message for months. But it kept coming out as too stiff and formal, not what he wanted to say. He decided to try simply speaking to them as colleagues, pupils, and friends.

"Words cannot express all that is in my heart as I look out upon you today. I am especially glad to see so many of our precious alumni gathered in this hall. Some of you date back all the way to our 'Cellar College' days, when we were meeting in a single room under the American Mission offices. Many more of you were taught in the rented buildings in Weyfour Street, which one of my AMB colleagues described as a 'rat-trap.'" A chuckle passed through the crowd.

"We now list among our graduates many of the leading professionals in Adamu and throughout the provinces of Buraan. You are now pastors, teachers, doctors, pharmacists, engineers, musicians, writers, translators, editors, lawyers, business leaders, government officials, to name but a few—also, masters in this very College. I am proud to say that I know several who have given generously of their time to mentor young students and graduates in their occupations. A wise soul once said that after we have passed through the door of opportunity, we must reach back and help others through the same door. And it gratifies me to know that our alumni are ready to do just that."

David felt that the whole day thus far was simply going *too* well. As he scanned the crowd, he did not see a single person disrobing in public, nor anyone flying into a racist rage. No one was having a sudden accident or a heart attack. No one was committing a crime or an act of violence. He braced himself for the inevitable.

"As you all know, our aim in the pursuit of a Christian higher education is not only to build strong and useful men. It is to develop good and moral men, proficient in clean, diligent, unselfish daily living. Our desire is that anyone meeting a Hardy College graduate in the future will recognize him simply by his honest and idealistic manner of behavior. All of you are capable of becoming such men, and we intend to help you achieve it.

"I once believed that we could advance the knowledge of God by sharing the corpus of Western science and civilization with less accomplished peoples. The theory was that all truth is one—thus, learning facts of science would perforce bring us nearer to the Author of all truth. But now, we have seen to what degree the perversion of Western societies threatens the world. In the Great War, we witnessed the astounding violence and waste of which we are capable. The guilt of supposedly advanced Western nations is appalling... to our lasting discredit. And here in Buraan during the War and deportations, we saw individuals who gave their utmost to help others, and those who sought to increase chaos and suffering for their own ends. Men and women of all nationalities, races and creeds. It is abundantly clear that the boundaries of moral and immoral behavior do not run between countries or civilizations, but pass through each individual human heart."

David paused a moment. He had not actually intended to say any of that.

"It should be *no* part of our mission to Americanize or Europeanize any of the peoples of this region. Nor may we covet any part of their territory, as some of the Great Powers indeed have done. What we must do is prepare you, the youth of Buraan, to develop and lead your nation in the interest of the nation itself. Perhaps even to equip you to act in self-defense *against* the pernicious influences likely to invade from the West: militarism, atheism, permissive social customs. To do this, you will need to use the instruments of a higher education that is sound, modern, and competent in using power wisely. And to attain this without losing your souls, it must be thoroughly permeated with the sacrificial spirit of Christ."

He now had everyone's undivided attention.

"Does that mean we are trying to shape you into little religious duplicates of ourselves? No, it does not. Allow me to quote the words of Dr. Daniel Bliss, founder of the Syrian Protestant College: 'This College is for all conditions and classes of men without regard to color, nationality, race, or religion. A man white, black, or yellow; Christian, Jew, Mohammedan or heathen, may enter and enjoy all of the advantages of this institution for three, four, or eight years; and go out believing in one God, in many gods,

Chapter 12

or in no God. But it will be impossible for anyone to continue with us long without knowing what *we* believe to be the truth and our reasons for that belief.

"Hardy College stands unequivocally within the stronghold of the evangelical Christian faith and life. Openly and earnestly, we must present our belief with tact and with tenderness, never in a spirit of superiority or the destructive depreciation of the faith of others. When you leave us, I want you to be able to say that Reverend Galloway served you in Christian love, and gave you the tools to become in turn a man for others, adept at every good work. Thank you."

The end of the address was a signal to Mauris Agarin at the piano, who opened the stirring strains of *Guide Me, O Thou Great Jehovah*. The boys all rose, and with them the rest of the assembly. They sang with the energy of youth, "Songs of praises, songs of praises, I will ever give to thee . . . I will ever give to thee."

At the end of the hymn, Suzanna Hardy came forward and presented greetings from the Board in the United States and the donors she had marshaled into the support of the College. David remained on the podium and admired her as she spoke. She was wearing a perfectly tailored pearl-gray suit, with perfect little matching gray leather boots and a perfect little matching gray felt hat. Whatever the occasion, she always looked perfect. He had to remind himself actually to listen to what she was saying.

"So now, we can offer to today's students a physical facility equal to the intellectual and spiritual richness of the College environment. And of course, apart from the ways many of us have been able to add to this effort, let us be clear: the success of this College is due to one man, the Reverend David Galloway. He has given us twenty-seven years of vision, commitment, love, and service. For this reason, and with the consent of our local Board of Management and the Board of Oversight in the United States, I wish to announce that henceforth this wonderful school shall be known as Galloway College. Incorporated in the state of Pennsylvania and resident in the Kingdom of Buraan!"

There was a silence for the space of a single breath, and then rampant applause from the audience. Suzanna turned to him to see the result of her announcement, and found David staring at her as though he had suddenly gone deaf. Seeing that she was not likely to obtain a satisfactory response from him, she continued.

"Boys of the College, please stand." They all did so. "My dears, there is a tradition in Britain's Royal Navy that the crew of a certain battleship call themselves by the name of that ship. If the ship is the H.M.S. Exeter, the crew will proudly proclaim, 'We are Exeters!' I ask you now to tell us who you are, in the same way. 'We are Galloways!'"

The boys caught on to this idea immediately. "We are Galloways!" they shouted. And again and again, "We are Galloways! We are Galloways!"

Rejoicing spread through the room, and everyone who understood what was going on quickly explained it to those who were confused. People in the room laughed and hugged each other. Through it all, David sat like a statue, unable to react.

He was relieved by Mr. Agarin boldly launching into the recessional hymn: *Praise, My Soul, the King of Heaven*. The people flowed out to the school courtyard, and as they did so, their ears were thrilled by the pealing of the new tower bell. The strike note of E, with its related harmonic tones. E . . . E . . . E . . . with several seconds of reverberation in between. The boys were hopping up and down with excitement, and many of the grownups were unabashedly delighted as well. People could catch glimpses of the sun flashing from the polished bronze bell as it swung, enjoying the unexpected entertainment.

Last to leave the building came David and Suzanna. She led him by the hand, still stunned, emerging to the sound of the ringing bell and the cheering people, like a newly married couple coming out of church from their wedding ceremony. Well-wishers crowded around to congratulate him. Manro Olorzey, chairman of the local Board, embraced him like a brother. It seemed that everyone had conspired to surprise the consensus-builder with this *fait accompli*.

Working gradually through the crowd, Suzanna steered David toward the front gate of the campus. Most of the crowd moved with them. As they approached the gate, he saw that Hooley and Brinkwater had finished their work and cleared away the wooden barrier.

They had constructed a handsome stone entryway flanking the iron gate. And affixed upon one side of the stone structure was a large bronze

Chapter 12

plaque with raised lettering: GALLOWAY COLLEGE. The crowd responded again with assent and applause.

David turned then to Suzanna, and saw her radiant with happiness. She knew that her very involved gambit had proved a resounding success. His heart melting, he embraced her, right there in front of everyone.

As he held her close, his lips were just beside her ear. "Suzanna," he whispered. "My beloved Suzanna, will you marry me?"

"Of course I will, you daft old thing," she whispered back. "We've waited long enough, I think."

The throng was not eager to leave the scene of so much pomp and pleasure. But eventually the guests departed, the boys went off to do boy things with their free time before the start of classes on the next day, and the evening cooled into an indigo calm.

David had lived so long with professional and personal struggle—and endured so many stunning setbacks—that he scarcely knew how to absorb the experience of a single flawless day.

That week in September was not the end of David's story, of course. He and Suzanna did marry, despite the obvious challenges of reconciling their radically different approaches to life. She was reluctant to give up her passion for glamorous travel, but the decision was made for her in short order, when she almost immediately and surprisingly found that she was expecting their child. As an "elderly primigravida" over the age of 35, hers was a high-risk pregnancy, and Dr. Dillon ordered a lengthy confinement and much bed-rest. At the appointed time, she brought forth their child, a son, and they named him Joseph Hardy Galloway.

The little heir's substantial fortune took a blow in the Wall Street crash of 1929, but recovered nicely when demand for steel skyrocketed during World War II.

While Suzanna was confined in her luxury suite at the Windsor Hotel, Mr. Hooley and Mr. Brinkwater built for them a comfortable new house in Adamu. No one expected her to move into David's poky little rooms in the American Mission building. While Joseph was very young, she stayed close to home, but eventually they had the fun of showing him the world. And Suzanna finally got the chance to take David to Egypt for an extended visit, to see the campus of Assiut College and the treasures that had recently emerged from King Tutankhamun's tomb.

A few weeks after the convocation at Galloway College, David received the letter from Jadali Veego. At once he threw himself into the effort to trace Shueyda Momonen and then get him out of prison. David exerted every ounce of the political capital he had acquired over the years; the American Ambassador got tired of hearing Galloway's name. At least there was an American Ambassador in Buraan by then, and not only in remote and indifferent Constantinople.

Like most of the persons denounced by informers and arrested in Buraan, Shueyda had no actual crime to answer for. So after nearly two years of misery and intimidation, he was released to make room for more.

Shueyda returned not to Adamu, but to Charga. David was unable to persuade him otherwise. He married Jadali Veego and adopted her son Arrun as his own. And against all odds, their house became the nucleus for a new Christian community. The experience of oppression was a potent stimulant for the growth of the church; those who felt alienated from their own society found a home there. The music lovers of Charga were irresistibly attracted to worship. Some fellow inmates to whom he had offered emotional and spiritual support while in prison sought him out later and joined them. Before long, they were in the process of building a little church, and as the Holy Spirit would have it, Shueyda at last became the duly installed and appointed pastor of the Charga congregation.

David officiated at Shueyda's installation. He assisted in the dedication of the new Charga church building. And he baptized all of the adorable Momonen children.

And when in due course David Galloway suffered the cerebral hemorrhage that ended his life, it was Shueyda who read for him the Order for the Burial of the Dead. And at the funeral—a massive event attended by half of Buraan—Shueyda sang this:

> What a wonderful salvation
> Where we always see his face
> What a peaceful habitation
> What a quiet resting place.
>
> See, a fruitful field is growing

Chapter 12

Blessed fruits of righteousness
And the streams of life are flowing
In the lonely wilderness.

Blessed quietness . . . holy quietness
What assurance in my soul
On the stormy sea, speaking peace to me
How the billows cease to roll.

David Galloway's body was committed to the earth in the American Mission cemetery at Adamu, beside those of Mary Dale and little Anne. Shueyda suggested, and Suzanna agreed, that on his stone should be inscribed: *Let the Mercy of the Lord Our God be Upon Us, and Establish Thou the Work of Our Hands.*

Selected Sources

Allsebrook, Mary and Anne Allsebrook. *Born to Rebel: The Life of Harriet Boyd Hawes.* Oxford: Oxbow, 2002.
"American Women in Peril at Hadjin." *The New York Times,* 23 April 1909.
Assiut College, American Mission, Assiut, Egypt. Cairo: W. Abu Fadil's Printing Press, 1925. Pamphlet in the Special Collections of Princeton Theological Seminary.
Barton, James L. *Daybreak in Turkey.* Boston: Pilgrim, 1908.
———. *Status and Outlook of Missionary Work in Turkey: A Review of Conditions in the Near East.* Boston: American Board of Commissioners for Foreign Missions, 1924.
———. *The Story of Near East Relief (1915–1930): An Interpretation.* New York: Macmillan, 1930.
The Book of Common Worship. Philadelphia: Presbyterian Board of Publication, 1906.
"Brooklyn Man Saw Missionaries Shot." *The New York Times,* 2 May 1909.
Calvin, Jean. *Institutes of the Christian Religion.* Vol. XXI, book IV, ch. XX. Edited by John T. McNeill. Translated by Ford Lewis Battles. Philadelphia: Westminster, 1960.
Catalogue of Central Turkey College at Aintab. Constantinople: Bible House, 1901.
"The Drug Store Laboratory." *National Association of Retail Druggists (N.A.R.D.) Notes* 7/17 (28 January 1909) 12.
Dulles, Charles W. *Accidents and Emergencies: A Manual of the Treatment of Surgical and Medical Emergencies in the Absence of a Physician.* 7th ed. Philadelphia: P. Blakiston's Son & Co., 1910.
Elliott, Mabel Evelyn. *Beginning Again at Ararat.* New York: Fleming H. Revell, 1924.
Evans, E.W. Price. *Timothy Richard: A Narrative of Christian Enterprise and Statesmanship in China.* London: Carey, [1952].
Fisher, Daniel W. *Calvin Wilson Mateer: Forty-Five Years a Missionary in Shantung, China.* Philadelphia: Westminster, 1911.
Fleming, Daniel J. *Whither Bound in Missions.* International Committee of the YMCA. New York: Association Press, 1925.
Genovese, E.N. "Paradise and Golden Age: Ancient Origins of the Heavenly Utopia." In *The Utopian Vision: Seven Essays on the Quincentennial of Sir Thomas More,* edited by E.D.S. Sullivan, 9–28. San Diego, CA: San Diego State University Press, 1983.
Gingeras, Ryan. *Fall of the Sultanate: The Great War and the End of the Ottoman Empire, 1908-1922.* Oxford: Oxford University Press, 2016.
Graham, Carol. *Azariah of Dornakal.* London: SCM, 1946.
Hamlin, Cyrus. *My Life and Times.* Boston: Pilgrim, 1893.

Selected Sources

Hess, Julius Hays. *Premature and Congenitally Diseased Infants*. Philadelphia: Lea & Febiger, 1922.

Hodge, J.Z. *Bishop Azariah of Dornakal*. Madras: Christian Literature Society for India, 1946.

Hogg, Rena L. *A Master-Builder on the Nile: Being a Record of the Life and Aims of John Hogg, D.D., Christian Missionary*. Pittsburgh: United Presbyterian Board of Publication, 1914.

Hutchison, William R. *Errand to the World: American Protestant Thought and Foreign Missions*. Chicago: University of Chicago Press, 1993.

Hyatt, Irwin T. *Our Ordered Lives Confess: Three Nineteenth-Century American Missionaries in East Shantung*. Cambridge, MA: Harvard University Press, 1976.

Jessup, Henry Harris. *Fifty-Three Years in Syria*. Vol. II. New York: Fleming H. Revell, 1910.

Jones, E. Stanley. *The Christ of the Indian Road*. New York: Abingdon, 1925.

Kerr, Stanley E. *The Lions of Marash: Personal Experiences with American Near East Relief, 1919–1922*. Albany, NY: State University of New York Press, 1973.

Khoury, Ghada Yusuf. *The Founding Fathers of the American University of Beirut: Biographies*. Beirut, Lebanon: American University of Beirut Press, 1992.

Kreyenbroek, Philip G. *Yezidism—Its Background, Observances and Textual Tradition*. Lewiston: Edwin Mellen, 1995.

Kunzler, Jakob. *In the Land of Blood and Tears: Experiences in Mesopotamia During the World War, 1914–1918*. Arlington, MA: Armenian Cultural Foundation, 2007.

Lambert, Rose. *Hadjin and the Armenian Massacres*. New York: Fleming H. Revell, 1911.

Macfarlane, Norman C. *Ian Macfarlane: Soldier and Medical Missionary*. London: Religious Tract Society, 1922.

Machen, J. Gresham. *Christianity and Liberalism*. New York: Macmillan, 1923.

———. "Machen to Mother." Letters in the Special Collections of Westminster Theological Seminary, 5 October 1913 and 10 October 1913.

Mateer, Calvin W. "The Relation of Protestant Missions to Education." *Records of the General Conference of the Protestant Missionaries of China, held at Shanghai, May 10-24, 1877*. Shanghai, China: Presbyterian Mission Press, 1878.

Miller, Donald E. and Lorna Touryan Miller. *Survivors: An Oral History of the Armenian Genocide*. Berkeley, CA: University of California Press, 1993.

Moorshead, R. Fletcher. *The Appeal of Medical Missions*. Edinburgh: Oliphant, Anderson & Ferrier, 1913.

Morgenthau, Henry. *Ambassador Morgenthau's Story*. New York: Doubleday, 1918.

Munro, John M. *A Mutual Concern: The Story of the American University of Beirut*. Delmar, NY: Caravan, 1977.

"Murder and Pillage Renewed at Adana." *The New York Times*, 28 April 1909.

National Association of Retail Druggists. *N.A.R.D. Journal*. 13 February 1919, 773.

Nelson, William S. *Silver Chimes in Syria: Glimpses of a Missionary's Experiences*. Philadelphia: Westminster, 1914.

Newbigin, Lesslie. *Mission in Christ's Way: A Gift, a Command, an Assurance*. New York: Friendship Press, 1988.

Noll, Mark A. and Carolyn Nystrom. *Clouds of Witnesses: Christian Voices from Africa and Asia*. Downers Grove, IL: InterVarsity, 2011.

Selected Sources

Nyhagen Predelli, Line. "Marriage in Norwegian Missionary Practice and Discourse in Norway and Madagascar, 1880–1910." *Journal of Religion in Africa* 31/1 (February 2001) 17–48.

Pickett, J. Waskom. *Christian Mass Movements in India: A Study with Recommendations.* New York: Abingdon, 1933.

Proposals for Establishing a Christian College and Medical School in Central Turkey. Aintab: Central Turkey College, 1872.

Rao, R.R. Sundara. *Bhakti Theology in the Telugu Hymnal.* Bangalore, India: Christian Institute for the Study of Religion and Society, 1983.

Riggs, Alice Shepard. *Shepard of Aintab.* New York: Interchurch Press, 1920.

Robert, Dana L. "The First Globalization: The Internationalization of the Protestant Missionary Movement Between the World Wars." *International Bulletin of Missionary Research* 26/2 (April 2002) 50–66.

Salt, Jeremy. *Imperialism, Evangelism and the Ottoman Armenians, 1878–1896.* New York: Routledge, 1993.

Sharkey, Heather J. *American Evangelicals in Egypt: Missionary Encounters in an Age of Empire.* Princeton, NJ: Princeton University Press, 2008.

Speer, Robert E. *The Non-Christian Religions Inadequate to Meet the Needs of Men.* Address before the Fifth International Convention of the Student Volunteer Movement, 1 March 1906.

Spon, Ernest. *American Library Edition of Workshop Receipts: Being a Complete Technical Encyclopaedia in Five Volumes.* 2nd ed. New York: Spon & Chamberlain, 1903.

Stanley, Brian. *The World Missionary Conference, Edinburgh 1910.* Grand Rapids: William B. Eerdmans, 2009.

Taneti, James E. *Caste, Gender, and Christianity in Colonial India: Telugu Women in Mission.* New York: Palgrave Macmillan, 2013.

Tarbell, Martha. *Tarbell's Teachers' Guide to the International Sunday-School Lessons for 1910.* New York: Fleming H. Revell, 1910.

Thomas, Frank W. "Albuminuria in Pregnancy." *The Southern California Practitioner* 21/8 (August 1906) 399–404.

Ussher, Clarence D. and Grace H. Knapp. *An American Physician in Turkey: A Narrative of Adventures in Peace and in War.* Boston: Houghton Mifflin, 1917.

White, George E. *Charles Chapin Tracy: Missionary, Philanthropist, Educator.* Boston: Pilgrim, 1918.

Whitehead, Henry. *National Christianity in India.* Madras, India: Christian Literature Society for India, 1911.

World Missionary Conference. "Mohammedan Lands in the Near East." *Report of Commission III: Education in Relation to the Christianisation of National Life.* New York: Fleming H. Revell, 1910.

Yates, Timothy. *Christian Mission in the Twentieth Century.* Cambridge: Cambridge University Press, 1994.

Yücel, İdris. "An Overview of Religious Medicine in the Near East: Mission Hospitals of the American Board in Asia Minor (1880–1923)." *Journal for the Study of Religions and Ideologies* 14/40 (Spring 2015) 47–71.

www.ingramcontent.com/pod-product-compliance
Lightning Source LLC
Chambersburg PA
CBHW050825160426
43192CB00010B/1899